D1871147

LEADERSHIP JOURNEY
A Practical Guide for Quantum Leap to Your Leadership

P/B = Market price of each share/ (Total assets - Intangible assets - Total liabilities) of each share

Or, Market price of each share / Owner's equity (or Book value of each share)

P/B value of less than one means either the company is undervalued or there is something fundamentally wrong with the company. A P/B ratio of greater than one indicates that the company has created wealth for its shareholders.

Price-to-Cash Flow (P/CF)

P/CF is a ratio that is a measure of the market expectations of a firm's future health:

P/CF = Share price/ Cash flow per share

The higher the ratio, the more expensive a company is considered. Sometimes, investors use free cash flow in the denominator rather than cash flow (free cash flow is cash flow minus capital expenditure).

4.1 Return on Equity and Return on Assets: Roles Played by Operations, Sales, and Finance

One of the basic obligations of a company's management is to increase (maximise) shareholder value by making good operating, sales, and financing decisions. From a financial perspective, the company's management decisions or performance can be scrutinised by analyzing return on investment (ROI) as return on asset (ROA) or return on equity (ROE). ROA is important to assess management's performance, while ROE is important from the owner's point of view. For our discussion, let's start with ROE.

ROE = Net Profit/ Equity = (Net profit/ Asset) × (Asset / Equity)

Or,

ROE = ROA × Degree of leverage

ROA is net profit/asset and leverage is asset/equity. It shows

ROE is higher than ROA due to the benefit of leverage (asset/equity greater than one due to the impact of debt employed in the business).

The above ROE formula can provide a lot of insight into the management's decisions and performance if the formula is broken down into its components, as first time shown by Du Pont's engineer Donald Brown.

ROE = (Net profit / Sales) × (Sales / Asset) × (Asset / Equity)

ROE = Profit margin × Asset turnover × Degree of leverage

Note that

- profit margin is dependent on operating decision.
- asset turnover is dependent on investment decision.
- degree of leverage is dependent on financial decision.

The above formula is also known as DuPont's formula. By way of this formula, we are able to show more explicitly how operating, investment, and financing decisions impact ROE or the overall performance of the management.

The profit margin is dependent on the operating decisions of the management. Profit is revenue minus cost. Revenue depends on the price of the product and the volume sold. It means the revenue side of the profit margin depends on how effective the price management is done for the company's products, how much market share is captured by the company's product, and how much product volume is sold. Manufacturing cost also depends on the operating decisions of the management (e.g., how reliable operating equipment is, how well raw material cost is managed, how contractor costs, as well as maintenance costs, are controlled, and how well labour expenses are managed).

Asset turnover is dependent on the investment decisions of the management. Asset turnover is sales divided by assets. Sales effectiveness has a direct impact on asset turnover. Assets are the sum of fixed assets and working capital. How much fixed asset should be dedicated to operation is a management decision. The working capital included an inventory of raw materials, spare parts,

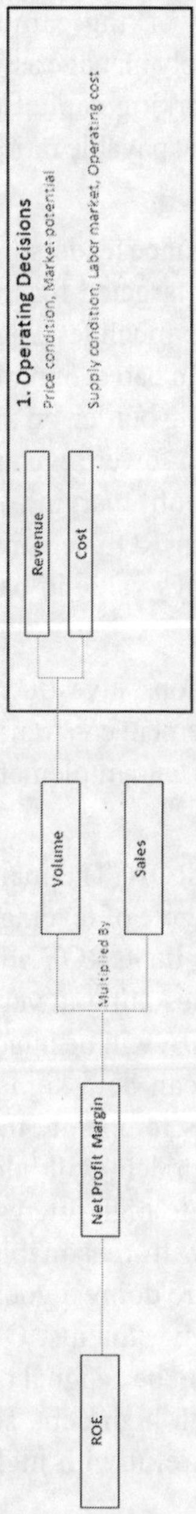

Fig. 4.1: Profit Margin: Operating Decision

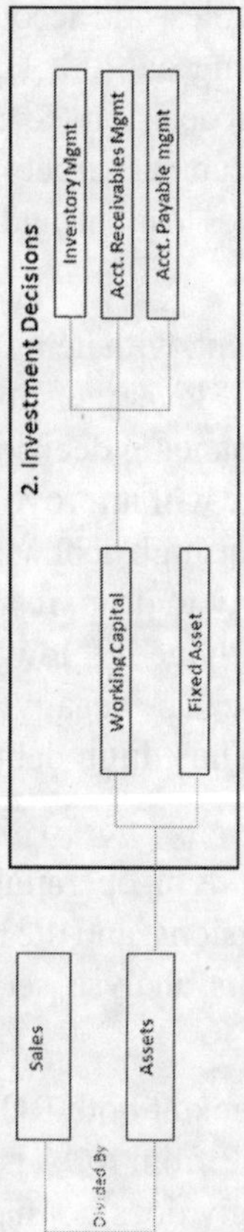

Fig. 4.2: Asset Turnover: Investment Decision.

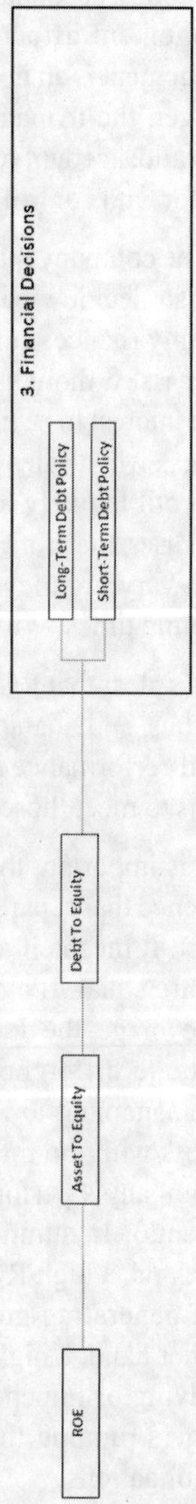

Fig. 4.3: Degree of Leverage: Finance Decision.

fixed goods, accounts receivables, and accounts payables. Inventory management affects working capital. Hence, working capital management is an investment decision. To effectively manage asset turnover, the management can set targets for working capital to asset ratio, account receivables to asset, and account payable ratios, monitor, and control.

The company management, with help from finance leadership, can also decide what kind of leverage should be targeted for the company (hence, this is a financing decision). Too much leverage will be risky, though leverage will improve ROE. In bad economic times, interest to be paid on the high debt will be a big burden on the business when sales are likely to drop, resulting in lower revenue (net profit is likely to take a huge hit, lowering profit margin). In some cases, the profit margin can be negative, making ROE negative due to very high leverage. Thus, high debt destroys value in bad economic times.

It is clear that ROE depends on operating decisions, investment decisions, and financing decisions, and the management can trend-related performance indicators, analyse, set targets, and implement actions to meet those targets.

It is important that we look at both ROE and ROA. The main difference that separates ROE from ROA is the degree of leverage or debt. It means if a company does not have any debt, ROE and ROA are equal. If a company has too much debt resulting in very high leverage, the difference between ROE and ROA will be huge. This huge difference between ROE and ROA can be a signal for management to review management decisions to operate the business with too much debt (as in bad times, high debt will hurt the company's performance to a great extent due to high-interest payments). In summary, if ROA is acceptable with reasonable debt levels, a high ROE indicates that managers are doing a good job of generating good returns on shareholder investments. On the other hand, a high ROE with very low ROA can be a signal of underlying or impending problems associated with high debt, so managers running the company must be extra careful with high debt obligations.

4.2 Economic Value and Enterprise Value

Executive Summary

Business professionals often make investment decisions to create value for the enterprise. The question for non-finance professionals is how to estimate economic value creation as a result of certain investments. This article presents methods to quantify economic value creation. Generally, it is assumed if an investment has a positive net present value or positive return on investment, the investment must be creating economic value. However, this might not be the case. Even a positive return on investment might be destroying economic value. Furthermore, the chapter presents simple methods to estimate enterprise value and increase the enterprise value based on economic value added as a result of certain investments. The article shows that each dollar of economic value creation will increase enterprise value several folds. These insights into economic value and enterprise value may be useful to non-business professionals, and they are likely to have a better appreciation of their investment decisions.

Economic Value

When we talk about adding value to the business, I always wonder what it really means and how to estimate it. How do we justify that our actions in the business have really created value? Many times, we take actions to address safety and environmental matters, and those are not necessary to create economic value. For strategic reasons, businesses make capital expenditures. For example, an old machine may be operating fine but may still have a risk of catastrophic failure due to its being worn out. If the machine fails and the lead time to replace the machine is long, a strategic decision could be to replace the machine (or its critical parts) before the catastrophic failure happens. At the same time, capital expenditure decisions are made to invest funds to increase the uptime (runtime) of the machine, rate the index of the production line, reduce energy consumption, or make a new product. The important question is how we should assess if these investments are creating value (or real wealth) for the business.

Before we get into specifics of economic value (or, in finance terms, economic values added [EVA]), let's take a simple example. Say, you borrow $2 million, start a business, and make a net profit of $150,000 per year. Is this investment creating value (or economic value)? If you invest this money in stocks, bonds, or a combination of these and expect to have a return of eight percent, you will make $160,000 per year sitting at home. So the real question is investing in the business if the value has been destroyed by at least $10,000 (it means the market could have created a higher return than my business did). Though your net income is positive, and the rate of return on this investment is 7.5 percent, your investment may still not be adding value or might not have created "true" wealth for yourself. The concept of EVA is very useful in assessing if a given investment creates value or not.

EVA helps us measure true wealth creation by taking into consideration both net operating profit created by the invested capital and the cost of capital employed. EVA is estimated as follows:

EVA = Net operating profit after tax - Cost of capital employed to generate this profit

= NOPA - (WACC × Economic capital employed)WACC is the weighted average cost of capital. Note that the capital is really a combination of debt and equity. Hence, the interest rate on debt and the cost of equity are both considered in estimating WACC. WACC is sometimes also known as the hurdle rate.

WACC = percent Debt (of asset) × Interest rate on debt + percent Equity (of asset) * percent Cost of equity

The cost of equity is the return on equity (ROE) of the company (it means the return the company is getting on its equity). It is interesting to note that even if a project may be financed at a much lower interest rate than the cost of equity, the EVA takes into consideration the true cost of capital to the investment (and this is what is referred to as the hurdle rate). It really means unless a project does not have a return higher than the hurdle rate, the project is really not creating value or wealth.

Example: Say a company can borrow funds at a 5 percent annual interest rate while the company's ROE is 20 percent. The company's asset includes 60 percent debt and 40 percent owner's equity. It means WACC = 60 percent debt × 5 percent interest + 40 percent equity × 20 percent cost of equity = 11 percent.

As interest on the debt will be tax deductible on the income statement, we can take its effect on WACC (assuming tax is 35 percent).

WACC = 60% × 5% (1 – 35% tax rate) + 40% * 20% = 9.95% (say 10%).

It means our investment in any projects in the company must have a return of more than 10 percent to create wealth (real profit) for shareholders, or our investment is destroying value and must not be pursued (unless, for strategic reasons, the company decided to pursue it).

Let's expand our example a bit further. Suppose, the management got approval for a $20 million project. Based on the operating profit (after tax) forecasts as a result of this project, the profit will be $4 million per year. How much EVA (real wealth or economic profit) will be created as a result of this investment? WACC for the company is 10 percent.

EVA = $4 million - ($20 million × 10%) = $2.0 million per year

EVA is positive. It means this project will create value for shareholders. For public companies, the market rewards this value creation very well by increasing the price of the company share (as earnings per share will improve as a result of this project or such projects that are creating value, the share price of the company will likely to improve, barring no other bad news for the company). The other very interesting question for managers (manufacturing in this case) is to ask if the real profit for the company due to this project has improved by $2.0 million per year, how the enterprise value (the price of the company if you sell it) will increase as a result of this good project. The answer to this question could be very obvious to finance people; however, it is important that non-finance managers (including plant heads, engineers, and project managers) learn these things and have a better appreciation of their efforts once they know what impacts their decisions are making on shareholder value and enterprise value. The next section discusses how enterprise value changes with economic value added.

Enterprise Value

It is intriguing and always interesting to learn how the buying prices of big and complex firms are estimated. Is it the asset value of the business or the market or book value of the business? Or should it be estimated by calculating the present value of the future cash flow streams of the business? If a business is making a net profit of, say, $20 million per year, what is the real worth of this business? In a simplistic way, one can assess the following way: to earn $20 million per year, you may ask how much money you must have in the market to earn $20 million as income (after tax). Assuming a 10 percent historical return from the market, we must have $200 million invested in the market to earn $20 million on this investment. At least this is a rough calculation. Now, one needs to ask how much asset is engaged to generate this profit of $20 million. Let's create some other numbers to continue our discussion. Based on the balance sheet of this, let's assume the business's total asset is $100 million, out of which $60 million is in total liabilities and $40 million in owner's equity. Again, assume this business has $10 million cash in the bank. This business is traded publicly, and its market capitalisation (total shares times the price of each share) is $80 million. What is the enterprise value of this business? As new owners, we have to own the business liabilities fully. It is obvious we will get the cash back when we buy this business. So the cash is helping to reduce my buying cost of the business (or reducing the enterprise value). It is also clear I should pay for the market capitalisation (this is the market value of owner's equity). The EV is thus calculated as follows:

EV = Market cap + Total debt (including all liabilities) + Minority interest and preferred shares – Total cash and cash equivalents

For the above example, the EV of the business = $80 million + $60 million + 0 - $10 million = $130 million (assuming minority interest and preferred shares to be sero).

Now, if a $130 million business is generating $20 million net profit, the return on EV is about 15 percent, which seems to be quite reasonable. Now, what happens if the market is excited about this business and the share price has gone up quite a bit for future higher earnings growth? As a result of this excitement, let's say the market capitalisation is $150 million. Assuming all other figures unchanged, the EV of this business now would increase by $70 million (market capitalisation increased from $80 million to $150 million) to $200 million. Now, if the business keeps giving only $20 million profit, the increased EV may not justify this kind of profit and punish the business by dropping the share price. Again, for finance people, these concepts and calculations may be obvious; however, I strongly recommend that non-finance managers and professionals of the company have a fair understanding of these concepts and calculations so they can have a better appreciation of the likely impacts their investment decisions may make on value creation and enterprise value.

Coming back to the question raised in the economic value added section, when the EVA is $2 million on a $20 million investment while operating profit has improved by $4 million, what is the impact of this on the enterprise value? Since the EVA is positive, the enterprise value must increase as well. The business invested $20 million in new plant assets. The project was financed by assuming new debt. It means the total debt component in the EV equation has gone up by $20 million. If the project did not create or destroy any value, at a minimum, the enterprise value of the business must increase by at least $20 million. As this project has created real economic value (EVA), the market capitalisation should be more now than before. But how much more?

A rule of thumb for non-finance managers could be based on the PE (price-to-earnings ratio) value of traded companies. Let's assume the average PE of the market is roughly eighteen. It means for one-dollar earning on each share, the price of the share will improve by eighteen dollars (eighteen times the earnings). We can use industry-specific PE value for this business to be more realistic in terms of estimating the increase in enterprise value of the business as a result of this project. Let's assume the industry-specific PE is 15 for this business. As the new project has resulted in a \$4 million net profit after tax (assuming after interest is paid on debt as well), the market capitalisation of this firm can be assumed to increase by \$60 million (\$4 million times fifteen). Whether the market will reward the company immediately for this performance improvement is a moot point (as the market may not realise the impact immediately or the company may not communicate this forecast right away).

The key point here for manufacturing and non-finance personnel is that when we show a sustainable improvement in net profit, the enterprise value increases by several times the increased profit. A \$1 million profit may increase enterprise value by \$15 million. If your company has been making \$20 million as net profit and you have initiated some programmes to increase this profit by new investment or cost-cutting efforts, or by launching new products and as a result, the projected net profit is \$50 million, the enterprise value of your business is very likely to increase by \$400–450 million (market capitalisation for \$20 million was estimated to be \$300 million, while now for \$50 million net profit is \$750 million, so \$50 times 15 based on a PE of 15). It means you and your team might have created a real enterprise value of \$400 million and must be congratulated. The challenge I see is that non-finance personnel, especially manufacturing personnel who are responsible for creating this value doesn't really connect their efforts with these results in the light of enterprise value. They will engage better if they can translate their efforts into the creation of economic value and enhancement of enterprise value many folds. It is therefore strongly suggested these finance basics must be taught to all engineers, project managers, and manufacturing leaders.

I would like to have a quick note on the matter of estimating enterprise value based on EBITDA (earnings before interest, tax, depreciation, and amortisation). In the above example, for simplicity, we used PE value to assess the increase in market capitalisation of the business. The net profit of the company will depend heavily on the company's debt structure (if highly leveraged, heavy interest will be paid, and this will reduce the company's net income). Also, the impact of depreciation and amortisation may skew the company's net income. Hence, it is fair to estimate EBITDA rather than use a multiplier to assess the company's future market capitalisation. Depending on the industry, this factor could vary from as low as six to fifteen (for slow-growing industries to fast-growing industries). Note that for a potential buyer, the lower the multiplier, the lower the purchasing price (enterprise value of the business).

4.3 Decision on Capital Investment

One of the main responsibilities of operation managers and senior executives of the company is to analyse and allocate capital funds to maintain or grow the operation. Project managers and engineers may have to put together the capital expenditure requests after their technical analysis indicates a project to be feasible technically. Analyzing these capital fund requests is a crucial exercise for these leaders. capital expenditures may be needed for the following reasons:

- Safety and environmental projects
- To maintain operation, replace a worn-out or damaged component or equipment (capex to maintain)
- Expansion of the existing product line or installation of new process equipment for the new products (growth capex)
- Cost reduction projects

While safety or environmental projects may not require financial analysis, other projects may require close financial scrutiny. Capital expenditure is important for the continued prosperity or growth of any business. Capital expenditures are generally long-term investments and involve a lot of risks due to uncertainties associated with the financial benefits these investments will bring. These uncertainties may be due to any or all of the following reasons:

- Uncertainty in the timing of the investment
- Potentially changing conditions for the product over the project life, causing much lower financial benefits (product price may drop, resulting in a much lower return than projected on the investment)
- Unexpected changes in the economic condition during the lifetime of the project

Once a capital investment is made, it is not easy to change business decisions about the investment. It has been seen time and again many capex projects do not meet their commitments relative to improvements in production or availability of the equipment. It seems project managers often overcommit themselves in the hope of receiving management approval for the projects. In such cases, the credibility of the managers responsible for the implementation of the project gets hurt. Hence, strong advice to all project managers is not to overcommit. Your credibility as a project manager will hurt a great deal if your projects are overcommitted and do not meet agreed-upon objectives. A project must be financially attractive for the management to approve funding. The following financial assessment tools are used to assess the capex projects:

1. Payback period
2. Net present value (NPV)
3. Internal rate of return (IRR)

The payback period is the time required to recover the original investment. The payback period gives managers a quick idea of whether the original investment will be recovered within the life span of the project. The payback period is calculated as follows:

Payback period = Original net investment / Average annual operating net cash flow

Net cash flow is the difference between cash inflows and outflows due to this investment. For example, cash inflows may include increased sales and reduced operating costs, while cash outflows include items such as increased labour expenses, increased consumption of materials, and increased fuel and electric costs. Operating net cash flows should really be calculated after taxes to get a realistic picture of the payback period. Suppose a net investment of $500,000 provides $150,000 net cash flow after taxes, the payback period is then 3.5 years. Before taxes, the net cash flow will be $230,000 if the tax rate is 35 percent. Based on a net cash flow of $230,000, the payback period will be 2.2 years, which is misleading. Though the payback technique is very simple and intuitive, the technique does not consider economic returns after the payback period. Some projects may have lower returns in the beginning years. In such cases, the payback period technique will not be a good technique to assess the economic benefits of the project.

A modified approach to estimate the payback period is to calculate the net cash flow for each year and then discount the cash flow by the project's cost of capital. In this approach, the project's net cash flows are added until they sum to zero. A hypothetical case is presented:

Table 4.5: Net Cash Flow and Payback Period

Year	Net Cash Flow (annual), $	Discounted Cash Flow, $	Cumulative Sum, $
0	(500,000)	(500,000)	(500,000)
1	150,000	136,363	(363,637)
2	150,000	123,966	(239,671)
3	150,000	103,305	(136,366)
4	150,000	93,914	(42,452)
5	150,000	85,376	42954

The project cost of capital was assumed to be 10 percent. Year 2 net cash flow after discounting for two years at 10 percent rate is $150,000/ (1 + 10%) ^0.2 = $123,966.

Based on this modified approach, the payback period for the $500,000 investment is roughly 4.5 years. This method accounts for the time value of money and presents a more realistic picture.

The payback period approach, in spite of its drawback, is a useful management tool for assessing capital projects. These calculations are easy to perform. It is highly recommended that business managers, facility managers, project engineers, and managers familiarise themselves with this tool and have some idea about the project's payback period to make sound business decisions on capital projects.

Net Present Value (NPV)

The NPV approach is an improvement over the payback period approach for assessing capital investment projects. This approach relies on the discounted cash flow of future net cash flow streams. The cash flows are discounted at the project's "cost of capital." All the discounted cash flows are summed up. The project's initial investment is deducted from the sum of the discounted cash flow streams to calculate the net present value of this investment. If the NPV is positive, the project is providing excess return and is considered to be financially viable. An NPV of zero means the project cash flows are exactly sufficient to repay the invested capital and provide the required rate of return on that capital.

For example, the NPV of a $500,000 investment with $150,000 cash flow each year for ten years and 10 percent is the required rate of return (referred to as hurdle rate sometimes) is $421,687 (one can use a calculator to estimate the NPV of present capital investment).

Internal Rate of Return (IRR)

The IRR technique also uses discounted cash flow calculations. In this approach, the present value of all cash flows is calculated at a discounted rate, which results in the present value of cash flows being equal to the project's original capital expenditure. The discount rate is known as the internal rate of return of the project. Alternatively, we can say the IRR is the discount rate that results in the project's NPV of zero. For example, the IRR of a $500,000 investment with a $150,000 cash flow each year for 10 years would be 27.3 percent. It means if we discount future cash flows of $150,000 each year for 10 years, the NPV of all these future cash flows at a 27.3 percent discount rate will be exactly $500,000. The NPV of the project with a $500,000 investment would be thus zero dollars.

Whether the IRR is acceptable or not depends on the cost of the capital employed in the project. If the IRR exceeds the cost of the funds, we can say the project is financially attractive. Companies have many projects competing for funds. Ranking these projects based on IRRs is one way of deciding which projects to approve for funding. Furthermore, a company can decide to approve only those projects that provide a very high IRR (and not necessarily just above the cost of capital). The IRR technique is very powerful and intuitive (and superior to other techniques). The shortcoming of the IRR is, though, its assumption that all future cash flows available can be reinvested at the rate of IRR. For example, if the IRR of a project is 30 percent, then the inherent assumption in the IRR calculations is that the company will be able to reinvest this cash available in different years at a 30 percent rate of return. If this is not realistic, then the IRR for the project is an overestimation. Management must take caution in IRR interpretation, especially when IRR is much higher than 25 percent–30 percent.

4.4 How Healthy is a Company Financially?

I always wonder, and I am sure so do other leaders as to how to assess the financial health of a company. It could be the company one may be purchasing or investing in, or lending to, or it could be the company one may be joining as an employee. I made my own career mistake in this regard when I left a highly rewarding and promising job and joined a company that offered me a much higher pay and responsibility only to find out very soon that the company was in much deeper financial distress than I was made to believe. I soon left the company while this company filed for bankruptcy within a few months after I had joined. This company was not publically traded and I did not have easy access to their financial data. I take inspiration from this very tough personal experience to include this chapter on how we can assess the financial health of a company as a leader of that company or as an investor, lender, or as a potential employee.

Financial statements are available to give us various figures from the balance sheet, income statement, and cash flow statement. We have key financial indicators such as return on equity, return on asset, profit margin, EBITDA margin, debt-to-equity ratio, working capital, and so forth available to us to perform our own analysis of the financial health of the company. If it is a publicly-traded company, other indicators such as P/E (price-to-earnings ratio) and Price to Sales (P/S) of the company are available as well. Business professionals perform their own analyses using various indicators and assess a company's financial health. For non-finance professionals, and especially for manufacturing managers, engineers, and project managers without financial background (or active use of financial concepts), it becomes a bit confusing and overwhelming to analyse and understand the realistic financial health of the company. The irony is plant personnel are not exposed by the company to financial tools or analysis reports to get educated on these issues. As a result of this, at the plant level, there is a severe lack of understanding of financial matters, and they remain in the dark as to how the company's financial health is and how they can help to improve the performance if needed. It is very important for companies to educate their managers and future leaders of the company on such matters, so they can better appreciate the company's performance, understand and predict if there is any red flag, and can help in their own areas of influence.

To have a reasonably good understanding of the financial health of a company, a very powerful and easy-to-use tool is available. This tool is referred to as the Z-score formula. Though this tool is mostly used to predict the financial health of a company relative to its risk of going into bankruptcy within the next two years, the tool is also helpful to assess if the company's overall health score (Z-score) is high against some benchmark, and if it is so, business managers will have a good idea about the health of the company. The Z-score is used for the creditworthiness of the company. The Z-score formula was developed in 1968 by Edward Altman, an assistant professor at New York University at that time. This formula is widely used now. For publicly traded and non-publicly traded manufacturing firms, as well as for non-manufacturers and emerging markets, different versions of this formula are provided in the following:

For Public Manufacturing Companies:

$Z = 1.2\ T1 + 1.4\ T2 + 3.3\ T3 + 0.6\ T4 + 1.0\ T5$

Where,

T1 = Working capital/ Total assets

(Working capital is current assets – current liabilities)

T2 = Retained earnings/ Total assets

T3 = Earnings before interest and taxes (EBIT)/ Total assets

T4 = Market value of equity/ Total liabilities

T5 = Sales/ Total assets

Depending on the Z-score, the company's financial health can be described as follows:

$Z > 2.99$ "safe" zone, which means good health of the company

$1.81 < Z < 2.99$ "gray" zone, which means uncertain health

$Z < 1.81$ "distress" zones, which means the company's financial health is bad/may be in red (may go bankrupt in two years unless some drastic actions are taken to improve the score).

For Private Firms:

Z score is as follows:

$Z = 0.718\ T1 + 0.847\ T2 + 3.107\ T3 + 0.42\ T4 + 0.998\ T\ 5$

Where:

T1, T2, T3, and T5 are the same as above.

T4 = Book value of equity/ Total liabilities

$Z > 2.9$ safe zone

1.23 < Z < 2.9 gray zone

Z < 1.23 distress zone

For non-manufacturers and emerging markets

Z = 6.56 T1 + 3.26 T2 + 6.72 T3 + 1.05 T4

T1, T2, T3, and T4 are the same as defined above for publically traded firms.

Z > 2.6 “Safe” Zone

1.1 < Z < 2.6 “Gray” Zone

Z < 1.1 “Distress” Zone

A Brief Discussion on the above Financial Ratios:

T1 = Working capital / Total assets

This ratio measures liquid assets. The company in trouble will usually experience shrinking liquidity.

T2 = Retained earnings / Total assets

This ratio calculates the overall profitability of the company. Dwindling profitability is a warning sign.

T3 = EBIT / Total assets

This ratio calculates the current profitability of the company.

T4 = Market capitalisation/ Total liabilities

This ratio suggests how far a company's asset can decline before it becomes technically insolvent.

T5 = Sales / Total assets

This is the assets turnover ratio and is a measure of how effectively the company uses its assets to generate sales.

The Z-score is known to have 70 percent plus accuracy in predicting bankruptcies two years in advance.

Application of Z-Score to the Real-World Examples

We will discuss two examples to show how useful Z-score is in assessing a company's financial health. The first example is WorldCom taken from Investopedia to show the usefulness of Z-score in assessing the financial health of a company. WorldCom, Inc., the technical giant, was a high-flying company and inviting to investors in the late nineties and early 2000s. The company though collapsed in 2002, resulting in a loss of close to $100 billion for its investors. Its management was accused of cooking the books and falsely recording billions of dollars as capital expenditure rather than operating costs and thus inflated net profit.

Table 4.6: Z-Score Estimates for WorldCom, Inc.

Input	Financial Ratio	1999	2001	2002
T1	Working capital/Total Assets	-0.09	-0.08	0
T2	Retained Earnings/ Total Assets	-0.02	0.03	0.04
T3	EBIT/ Total Assets	0.09	0.08	0.02
T4	Market Value/Total Liabilities	3.7	1.2	0.50
T5	Sales/ Total Assets	0.51	0.42	0.30
Z-Score		2.5	1.4	0.85

As we note from the above Z-scores, the company was in the gray zone in 1999 and in a distressed zone in 2001. The company's performance kept deteriorating in 2002, and the Z-score fell to 0.85. The company filed for bankruptcy in 2002.

The second example is Bed Bath & Beyond, Inc., using its 2018 to 2022 financial data (finance.yahoo.com/quote/BBBY).

Table 4.7: Z-Score Estimates for Bed Bath & Beyond, Inc.

Input	Financial Ratio	2018	2019	2020	2021	2022 (8/31/2022)

T1	Working capital/Total Assets	0.34	0.20	0.25	0.07	0.02
T2	Retained Earnings/ Total Assets	0.55	0.31	0.27	0.05	-0.17
T3	EBIT/ Total Assets	-0.04	-0.30	-0.13	-0.26	-0.66
T4	Market Value/Total Liabilities	0.41	0.25	0.23	0.16	0.16
T5	Sales/ Total Assets	1.83	1.43	1.43	1.53	1.46
Z-Score		3.1	1.9	2.1	1.6	0.81

As we note from the above Z-scores, the company was in the safe zone (healthy) in 1999. However, the company was in the gray zone (uncertain health) in 2000 and 2001. The company, however, entered the distress zone with a Z-score of 1.6 in 2021. The deteriorating Z-score of 0.81 in 2022 shows the company's financial health weakened even further (recall, the distress zone means the company may go bankrupt unless the company takes some drastic actions to improve its financial performance). As of writing of this section of the book in January 2023, Bed Bath & Beyond is talking publically about filing bankruptcy.

Note that the Z-score is useful in assessing the relative financial health of a company. A deteriorating Z-score signals trouble ahead. If a Z-score indicates a problem, a more detailed analysis should be performed by qualified financial personnel to investigate specific problem areas, and then management must implement actions to address any matters of concern.

It is worth noting that for publicly traded companies, all required financial parameters to calculate Z-scores are available from the balance sheet and income statement of the company. These statements are available online for such companies.

Other Symptoms for Deteriorating Financial Health

Z-score certainly is a good indicator to assess the relative financial health of a company. I would like to advise manufacturing and other business leaders to pay attention to the trend of retained earnings also. If it is downward, it indicates the owner's equity is being destroyed by the management's decisions on new investment (the new investment does not have a return higher than the weighted average of the capital cost) or the way the routine business is being run. If the business continues to operate this way and the retained earnings keep deteriorating, there will be a time when retained earnings could be zero. If the company still manages to borrow capital and this capital still does not create real wealth, the owner's equity will be negative. In this case, the total assets of the company will be less than the total liabilities of the company. If this happens, it is then very likely the company will file for bankruptcy anytime soon (as the company may not be able to continue to borrow capital).

The trend of retained earnings is a lagging indicator of the financial health of the company. Some other symptoms of the deteriorating financial health of the company could be continued negative net profit, increasing amounts of accounts payables, inability to pay suppliers in a timely manner, and negative cash flow from operating activities (if the company's net income is less than the required capital expenditure to maintain the operation, the cash flow from operating activities will be negative). If this situation continues in this manner, and there is no new infusion of cash from external sources, the cash available to run the business will continue to dwindle. There will arrive a time when the company may not have enough cash available in its bank to make payments to suppliers or pay the salaries of the employees. This means the company may now be ready to file for bankruptcy.

4.5 Early Symptoms That Your Company Might be in Trouble to Operate

We talked about Z-score formula to assess the financial health of a company early. This is a very simple formula, and I strongly advocate that basic financial knowledge and the Z-score methodology must be learned by all key leaders of the manufacturing operation, especially for plant managers, operations managers, project managers, and process engineers. A Z-score trend analysis with a few years of data could be a good way to assess the relative and changing financial health of the company. In a publicly traded company, it will be easy to get financial data to calculate the Z-score of a company. In a privately held company, only a few top executives of the company will have access to financial statements, and other key players will not have access to this important financial information to perform their own independent analysis and question if the company is in good health or not. They have to rely on the top management to determine whether the company is in good health or not. The problem is one cannot fully rely on what is shared and told by the top management as there were numerous examples when the accounting books were falsified, and deliberately wrong information was shared with the market (WorldCom is just one example). In midsised and small companies, expertise may not be there to perform such analysis, or this kind of analysis may not be on the management's radar screen due to other focus areas.

In publicly traded companies, though the financial information is available to calculate Z-score, the challenge will be when, based on the Z-score, there are indications of possible trouble (if Z-score puts the company in the grey area). In this kind of situation, deeper analyses must be done to pinpoint problem areas. This exercise will be undertaken by finance experts. Operation personnel, on the other hand, will have symptoms in operation to indicate the problem. Unless these pieces (symptoms) of the "puzzle" are pulled together and viewed as a whole, one may still not understand the seriousness of the problem or if the actions taken by the management are working or not and turning the operation around for good. I will present symptoms from the manufacturing world that may give a good idea to operational personnel and others about the deteriorating health of the company.

The first and foremost symptoms in the manufacturing world are poor and deteriorating safety and environmental performance. A poorly managed company will start taking shortcuts and will not walk the talk on safety and environmental matters. It will struggle to fulfill its governmental obligations and start finding reasons and loopholes in the rules, regulations, and permit for not doing things right. This kind of company will rely more and more on external lawyers and consultants (to save millions of dollars of not doing the things, the company will pay lawyers and consultants, hopefully much less in the company's view, to make their case and drag issues with the authorities). The company officials will satisfy themselves by using arguments made by the company-paid lawyers and consultants that they are doing the right thing and justify in their minds that they are still complying or trying their very best to comply. Employees in the company will be advised to have all communication (however small) through lawyers only. Employees will be advised not to generate too many papers and emails on environmental and safety communication. Take a look at the company's safety performance (injuries, lost time incidents, and workman compensation) for the past few years, and we will either see the consistently poor performance (much worse than the industry's average) with no improvements at all or find the performance deteriorating (more first aid, reportable, and lost time injuries). You may want to check the company's incident investigation reports and learn if the company does sincere root cause analysis (RCA) on these incidents or if the incident report is a paper exercise just to comply with the law. An incident report with RCA, action log, and follow-ups will indicate a good safety culture. Otherwise, not having a good incident report on file with RCA and closure on the identified action is a serious symptom that the company's health (yes, even financial health) may not be good.

Another obvious and visible symptom that something is terribly wrong with the company is when you take a walking tour of the company's facilities, and you notice poor housekeeping prevails everywhere, and that is the culture of the operation (trash on roads, walkways, break rooms, and work areas). Main equipment may have too much dirt or oily build-ups and may not have been cleaned for years. Water may be leaking, and the ground around the leaking area may indicate that the leak may have been there for months, and nobody cares to address it. Coupled with this, if you notice employees in work areas are walking around without their personal protective equipment (safety glasses, hard hats, and boots) or they don't stop at the company's designated stop signs in the plant and don't wear safety seat belts. Also, you will not see many safety signs around, or if there are some around, they will be old, faded, or have build-ups. These all are very powerful symptoms of a very poor work culture, lack of pride in the workplace, and lack of accountability. This poor performance will not just limit to safety, you will notice that the overall work culture of the plant is very poor, and the plant operation performance will not be good either; rather, it will be historically deteriorating (take it as a one-to-one correlation). Hence, never ever ignore the safety performance and culture of your workplace. A good safety culture will bring discipline to the workforce, which will transfer to the overall work culture of the plant. This kind of operation has a much higher possibility of a successful operation).

Similarly, poor environmental performance and culture are a big concern for the overall health of the company. Some serious symptoms that are not a good reflection on the company's health, as I mentioned earlier, would be if even small internal environmental communication has to go through the company's lawyers or external lawyers, a serious sign that the company is not in good health. When environmental releases happen and the company does not document specifics to perform root cause analysis for fear of liabilities, it means something is not right with this company (it doesn't have the courage to be transparent and address the matter sincerely and openly). It means something is seriously wrong.

Another easy-to-monitor symptom is when neighbours call you about some problem they are experiencing due to your operation and would like your help to address the matter. If the company ignores such calls and does not investigate, internally is in defence mode with its staff, it means the company has a problem and is inviting more problems in the future. It reflects the closed style of management. A more serious symptom could be if you start ignoring inquiries by the authorities, and your lawyers will drag the issues with the authorities. When your lawyers and consultants start defending your position and do not advise you with sincerity and courage for the right actions, it means the company might be getting into more and more trouble. A great environmental culture with a mission of 100 percent compliance by all and full transparency will indicate you are a healthy company that is being run by trustworthy people with healthy mindsets. These people will create a lot of real wealth for the company. Ask yourself how your company is running and if there are symptoms or concerns. If yes, try to pull all these symptoms of safety and environment together, if you stay concerned, then dig deeper into other operation and performance issues. Most likely, you will find serious problems there as well.

Regarding operation, you must check out a few key performance indicators (KPIs). Such indicators may include production rate (say daily average), equipment runtime index (percentage time the equipment runs), mean time between failures (MTBF is a KPI that tells on average after how much time a given piece of production equipment goes down) of major equipment, maintenance cost or specific maintenance cost (maintenance cost per unit of production), and labour productivity (number of units or amount produced per labour hour). If the production rate of the main equipment is consistently dropping over some time (years), it is a symptom of concern. The daily rate must be trended to view it clearly. Otherwise, a few days of higher production will confuse operation staff, and they will keep thinking they can still produce as much as they used to do a few years ago. Similarly, trend availability or runtime of major equipment and check, if the trend is downward, is a concern. Similarly, if the MTBF trend is also downward, it means the equipment is breaking down more frequently now than it used to, and if it is so, it is a symptom of bigger problems. The maintenance cost trend is similarly an important indicator that will explain a lot about the operation. If the specific maintenance cost is increasing much faster than inflation over a period, it is a concern. If other KPIs (rate, runtime, MTBFs) are going in the wrong direction along with specific maintenance costs, it confirms that the operation has some serious problems on hand. Once these symptoms are identified, check if operation and maintenance analyse plant performance regularly using the right KPIs and perform RCAs regularly when the rate is lower than a certain threshold or when equipment breakdown happens and results in more than a small loss of production.

The quality of the products that we make is an important area of interest. One must check how quality is tracked and if there is a management system in place to address any unacceptable deviation in quality. Does the company have clear roles and responsibilities defined to monitor and manage the quality of its product? If this is not so, it is another symptom of a serious performance problem.

Check if the company has a good, reliable IT system to collect the operation and downtime data, or if the company performs all this manually. Does the company use a functional computerised maintenance system to manage its asset and maintenance? If in this day and age the company does not use software to track and analyse production and maintenance KPIs, it is a serious concern and does not bode well for the company's management and culture.

Other important symptoms of problematic operation include lack of accountability and lack of cost management culture. If the operation has not been performing well, does the leadership take action with specific assignments to people to address the issues? Or will the operation and maintenance teams just have casual or hallway talk about plant operation and move on without a specific action plan? If you go to a meeting with these plant personnel, do they come with specific, credible actions to follow and maintain an action log, or are these meetings daily coordination meetings and nothing more? If it is so, this is a symptom of a bigger performance problem.

If the company is not able to pay its suppliers in a timely manner, it could be another indicator of the company's financial health. If the suppliers are not being paid regularly and this situation is deteriorating over time, it is another good indicator that the company's financial health may be failing.

Manufacturing needs capital expenditure to maintain the equipment and operation. Without proper reinvestment in equipment, the equipment will age and not stay as reliable. As a result, the operation performance will start suffering, reflecting the adverse impacts on the rate index, runtime, and MTBFs. How much capex budget is needed to maintain is a very important question for managers to allocate appropriate funds for operation. It is very tempting for corporate management to reduce capex funds to improve the cash situation. In tough economic times, it is understandable that the operation might not have made as much profit, and so cash generation from the operation might have been reduced significantly. As a result, cash available for capex to maintain might be limited as well. However, if the average capex spend over a longer period (say, five years) is very limited, it is a concern for future operations. By not reinvesting in operations, the current management is pushing the responsibility and problem onto future management. After a certain time, if this practice continues, the equipment may suffer so much that bringing it back to acceptable condition may not be possible, and the only option left at that point is to secure funds to replace the equipment. If the economy during this time is bad and the company operation is now suffering because of unreliable operation, the company might find itself in serious trouble. Either you borrow funds (if you can) and replace the equipment and hope for a more reliable operation, or you may be forced to shut the door, depending on how the company's financial health is when all this is happening. This kind of challenge is not then limited to the replacement of one piece of equipment. There could be some equipment that may need replacement all at once. If the company decides to make these replacements in phases due to limited funds, the return on investment (improved performance) may not be realised until all key pieces of equipment are replaced (or bottleneck stays). The corporate leadership must realise when we don't reinvest the required funds to sustain the performance; the unreliable operation is likely to result in safety, environmental, and product quality problems. If it is so, government regulators may punish the company with sizeable financial penalties and force the company to address the issues on priority. The bad publicity in the press will tarnish the company's reputation. The workforce gets demoralised and may not be as engaged.

Hence, it is very critical for the company to ensure it reinvests proper funds to maintain its equipment and operation. A question that comes to mind is, on average, how much capex fund should be considered "appropriate" to maintain the equipment and operation. Different industries will have different methods to estimate the needed capex funds to maintain. Some companies will define this based on the cash available and allocate a percentage of cash available from operation to capex funds to maintain. Other industries may allocate capex funds based on the net profit earned by the company. As a simple rule, it seems the company should allocate the depreciated amount towards capex. However, depreciation is used in accounting for tax purposes and cash flow calculations and may not really be a true representation of the funds needed to maintain the facility. For example, when the facility is new, the depreciated amount will be significant. It does not mean, though, this new facility requires this depreciated amount to be reinvested. Does it mean this amount should be accrued for future years and allocated to capex funds in later years of the equipment's life? In some cases, the equipment's useful life may be thirty years or so. We can expect the equipment, with routine maintenance, to perform well for thirty years on average before requiring replacement. If it is so, it means in thirty years, we should have enough funds from depreciation available to be able to replace the equipment. It means roughly three percent of the equipment installed cost could be considered as allocation for replacement. If we reinvest these capex funds to maintain the equipment, it is very likely the life of equipment is extended many more years after thirty years. Let's take an example, say a new plant may cost $200 million today. If we have an identical old plant, it seems the capex funds to maintain could be close to $6 million. This is just one simplistic way to have a rough idea of what kind of capex funds may be needed to maintain the operation and equipment. There could be other ways to come up with the needed capex funds to maintain the facility. Remember, the capex to maintain is just one part of the total capex funds to operate the facility. The operation will require capex for safety and environmental projects. There could be capex needed to address product quality-related matters.

Other than capex allocation by corporate, capex management at the facility level must be checked to assess if the capex projects have been managed properly within the allocated time and budget and met the project objectives. Do these projects have clear project plans with goals and objectives, a defined budget, clear roles and responsibilities of individuals, a communication plan, and a risk mitigation plan? It may be wise to review a few projects completed in the last twelve months or so and make an assessment if the projects met their objectives and were completed as per the plan (if plans were prepared). Most times, it is seen there is no clear accountability among project team members to achieve certain outcomes of the project. If a project is funded based on the capex request that this project will increase or regain the lost rate by 5 percent, who is accountable for this increase after this project is done? Is it the project manager or the process team which did the calculations? If there are symptoms of poor safety and environmental culture, and deteriorating performance of operation and maintenance based on KPIs, there is a high possibility the project management will be of poor quality as well without accountability. The company might have allocated capex funds but did not achieve the promised results. If this is consistently so, poor project management is yet another serious symptom of a failing company.

4.6 Cash Is All That Matters

The goal of the management is to maximise long-term enterprise value. The ultimate value of any asset at the end of the day is the cash produced by the assets. Hence, the management goal as such should be to maximise cash flow from operations on a long-term basis. It should be noted by front-line operation managers and their teams that net income on the income statement is not the cash generated by the company at the end of the income statement period. This is because several items on the income statement are non-cash items and are used for accounting purposes. For example, depreciation is a non-cash charge that is deducted from the gross margin to get the net income. The depreciation should be added back to net income to obtain an estimate of cash flow from operations. An increase in working capital will deplete cash flow. Note that working capital is cash plus short-term investment plus accounts receivables plus inventories (of raw materials plus spare parts).

Similarly, capital expenditure will reduce cash flow. Furthermore, due to timing issues, operating cash flows can differ from accounting profits (or net income). Some examples are the following:

All the taxes reported on the income statement may not have to be paid during the current period or year.

Some sales may be on credit, so all sales will not represent cash.

Collecting accounts receivables or borrowing money will increase the cash amount.

Payment of interests, dividends, and accounts payables will cause cash to deplete.

Working capital: an increase will deplete cash flow

Capital expenditure will deplete cash flow.

The cash flow statement tells us how much real cash the firm has generated in a given period and how much cash the firm has in the bank at a given point in time. The statement presents a clear picture of the firm's ability to pay bills, creditors, and growth. No matter what the balance sheet and income statement show about the company's assets and net profitability, if a company runs out of cash and cannot meet its obligations, the company has to declare bankruptcy (so remember, cash is king, after all).

Remember, accounting books can be cooked, but the real cash in the bank will not lie. Hence, leaders of businesses must pay attention to the cash situation of the company. Operation leaders (including front-line managers in organisations) will make better business decisions when they really have a reasonably good understanding of the cash situation and financial statements. Hence, it is recommended that managers, engineers, and sales and marketing professionals are trained in the basics of finances (financial statements). It is alarming to realise that a big knowledge gap exists in the basic financial knowledge of front-line managers and leaders. A very small percentage only can relate to the basics of finances. Technical personnel is worse off in this regard. They are the ones who are largely responsible for creating economic value for the business. However, they are, in most cases, quite ignorant of how their work is being translated into financial statements. I believe once the technical personnel, as well as front-line managers (e.g., plant managers of manufacturing operations, engineers and other technical personnel, and sales managers of their regions), are trained on the basics of finances, including financial statements, they will be better decision-makers and help run businesses smarter and create higher economic and enterprise values.

Coming back to the cash flow statement, we must note that this statement provides transparency about the firm's performance. The income statement can be manipulated (for example, showing pending orders as revenue or increasing inventory and claiming increased inventory as sales revenue). Another way could be selling products on easy credits. The company, though, has sold the products but not received cash and may have sold the products to customers who may not be able to pay back. In this case, the income statement will look good, but unfortunately, the cash is not there for the goods sold. The cash flow statement, on the other hand, tells the true story of a firm's performance. The firm cannot do much to manipulate its cash situation (though some will still try, but will be caught relatively easily). Financial analysts can perform ratio analysis using figures from the cash flow statements and get insight into the firm's issues. For example, if the firm has reduced capital expenditures significantly to save cash, it may indicate the company's cash constraint situation. Also, avoiding capital expenditure may not be sustainable for long (or you drive the operation to the ground that will hurt the firm). If the cash from financing activities has increased suddenly, one could look into this matter further and check if the firm is using a lot more funds from its credit line.

A few words on operating cash flow and free cash flow: operating cash flow is defined as net income plus amortisation and depreciation plus the change in working capital minus capital expenditure. Note that working capital is cash plus short-term investment plus accounts receivables plus inventories (of raw materials plus spare parts).

Operating Cash Flow (OCF) = Net income + Amortisation or Depreciation – Changes in Working Capital – Capital Expenditure

Furthermore, free cash flow is different from operating cash flow in that free cash flow takes the effect of investment activities to arrive at the free cash flow (FCF) for the entity.

FCF = OCF + Net change in cash due to financial activities
FCF = OCF + Increase in notes payables and bonds - dividends paid to the shareholders

How Can Operations Help to Improve Cash Flow?

Maximizing OCF is the responsibility of operation managers. Operation managers can do the following three things:

- Cost management
- Reduce inventory
- Be selective in capex spend

Cost management is a very important responsibility of operation managers. It means they must identify different cost streams, understand their trends, question what can be reduced or eliminated, and then take action. Some of these cost items may include labour costs, maintenance costs, consultant costs, contractor costs, overtime costs, and so forth. A cost-reduction mindset and initiative will always find wasteful or avoidable spending. Right actions by operation managers will help reduce costs and improve cash flow.

Reducing inventory is a big part of reducing working capital. Inventory includes raw materials, spare parts, and finished goods. Any excess of any of these is a negative impact on cash flow. Inventory levels of these items must be tied to sales revenue. If sales are decreasing, inventory must be reduced. A reliable sales forecast will help optimise inventory levels. Obsolete inventory must be sold or written off. Critical spare parts inventory must be identified. Note that a reduction of x amount in inventory is an increase of x amount in cash flow.

Capital expenditure is another cash-depleting item. Capital expenditure may be needed to address safety and environmental compliance issues or overhaul the given machinery to prevent catastrophic failure. Capital expenditure may be needed to install new technology to improve operating line performance (runtime or capacity), resulting in an attractive rate of return on the investment. Operation managers must be aware of the impact of capital expenditure on cash flow. A good expenditure may help improve net income by way of increasing production or reducing cost, thereby having a favourable impact on operating cash flow. Maintaining machinery and equipment in good working condition will require capital expenditure, and a portion of total capital expenditure must be allocated to maintaining equipment and machinery (if we don't do so, the performance of operation will suffer a lot after some time of installation of the machine, hurting business and cash flow that time). Capital expenditure without attractive returns will adversely impact the operating cash flow of the business. Also, operation managers must know that capital expenditure, though, may not hurt the operation's net income (or earnings), except if its deprecation is recognised as cost on the income statement. However, if the capital expenditure has increased sales or reduced cost, these benefits may outweigh the depreciation, and overall, the capital expenditure may be beneficial. On the other hand, if capital expenditure is only to sustain the operation, the net income will reduce due to the increased amount of depreciation. Capital expenditure, though, is reduced from net income to calculate cash flow. Hence, capital expenditure decisions must be made carefully. Operation managers, though, must know that a high capital expenditure year after year may make cash flow streams from their units or operations lower and hence hurt the attractiveness of their operation for shareholders or senior leaders.

Free cash flow or FCF, by many, is considered to be a better indicator of a business's profit or ability to generate cash. FCF allows a company to pursue opportunities that enhance shareholder value. Without cash, the company will have a tough time paying dividends, reducing debt, making new acquisitions, and launching new products. Furthermore, it must be clear to non-finance managers that a net positive earning does not guarantee that the debt will be paid off or the interest payment obligations will be met if there is not enough cash on hand (again, net earnings can be manipulated by selling investments, but it does not reflect company's true performance).

In short, the cash flow statement must be analysed to see how much cash was generated from the operating activities, how much was used in investing activities, how much cash was needed to pay the debtor, and how much cash was borrowed by the firm.

5

Learn the Basics of Macroeconomics

I believe our leaders and managers (especially the upcoming ones) must have a good, basic understanding of the following aspects of macroeconomics. This know-how will help them relate their businesses in the larger context of the economy and global market.

5.1 GDP and the Key Factors that Influence It Most

Gross domestic product (GDP) growth has a direct influence on businesses. In an expanding economy with a growing GDP, businesses can be a bit more aggressive and grow with the economy, while in a shrinking economy with negative GDP growth, businesses have to cut expenses drastically and refocus on the revenue stream, market, and strategy. It will be useful for business managers to understand key factors that influence GDP growth (or the economy in which businesses are operating). (References: 1. www. investopedia.com, 2. The Main Determinants Affecting Economic Growth by Florin Teodor Boldeanau, Liliana Constantinescu, Bulletin of the Transilvenia University of Brasov Series V: Economic Sciences: Vol 18 (57) No. 2-2015, 3. MacroEconomics , Micheal Perkin. Growth Domestic Product, Chapter 5, 111-117, 4. Economic Growth, Feb 25 2022, Prateek Agarwal, www.intelligenteconomist.com).

GDP growth is mainly influenced by labour productivity and total hours worked by the labour workforce of a country. (GDP can be thought of as the multiplication of labour productivity times the size of the labour workforce). Labour productivity can be understood as the revenue generated by one labour hour in the country. It means, if labour productivity grows, real GDP per person grows as well (provided hours worked in a year do not decrease). Growth in total hours worked comes from the growing workforce. It means a shrinking labour workforce will shrink the real GDP as well (provided gains in productivity are higher than the reduction in the size of the labour workforce). If both labour productivity and the size of the labour workforce increase simultaneously, we can achieve faster growth in real GDP.

Now, one can ask how we increase labour productivity. The simple answer is we achieve a gain in labour productivity when we save and invest in physical capital (plants, equipment, and machines that generate revenue and increase revenue output per worker), increase the amount of capital per worker, and develop human capital by enhancing the skills and knowledge of the workforce or the people who will enter the workforce. It means investing in education and training of people to help increase labour productivity. Also, we do have gains in labour productivity when the workforce becomes more comfortable in their routine business (troubleshoots problems faster and addresses issues proactively) and thus, increase output (or GDP).

Innovation is another key factor that is a necessary ingredient in a country's culture to continue to improve labour productivity. Innovation means building and nurturing the country's education around innovation. This means investing in research and development by government and private entities (the actual realisation of return on R&D investment may take a long period of time, nonetheless, it is a must to achieve sustainable step-changes in productivity). The discovery of new technologies will enhance productivity. It means top-class school-level and college-level education, along with great universities with a big focus on R&D will be the key to a country's competitiveness in long run. Think about innovation (or revolution) in information technology in the last twenty years, allowing people and businesses to be more productive (new technologies emerged in businesses based on powerful internet, network, and communication tools, making business more productive. Artificial Intelligence, AI, is now helping further and likely to revolutionize the gains in productivity). Development in science and technology allows human beings to grow economic output many folds. For example, the outputs of food grains and other products increased many folds due to the use of new production methods and technologies in manufacturing.

Good infrastructure also helps grow GDP faster. Goods are moved faster from one place to another place with better infrastructure, increasing our productivity. R&D findings are translated into real business products by entrepreneurs. Hence, a culture that rewards entrepreneurship helps grow GDP faster.

The other key variable that greatly impacts real GDP is the size of our workforce. In the current age, due to unfavourable changes in demographics, the size of the workforce in many countries is shrinking (especially in European countries), putting great pressure on the growth of the real GDP of these countries. On the other hand, the large sizes of the workforce in countries such as China and India have become a great strength of these countries (technology has helped enhance workforce productivity along with the huge world market available to the economies due to the removal of trade barriers). This workforce will become an even further advantage for these countries if the workforce in these countries is educated and made skillful). No wonder then China and India are currently investing a large capital in the education and training of their workforce. The shrinking workforce of many developed economies will continue to be a concern as far as the growths of their economies are concerned. The old mindset that a smaller population is better so fewer people can be a lesser burden on limited natural resources and thus share the bigger size of the fixed size of the economic pie (Malthusian theory) may be questionable as long as innovation continues and natural resources are replenished, and environment is protected, so the growth is sustainable. Innovation in science and technology has increased the size of the economic pie for all. The revolution in agriculture productivity as a result of improved seeds, fertiliser, pesticides, and new technologies of farming allowed enhancing agriculture outputs many folds. New technologies have allowed new products in the market to enhance productivity. For example, automobiles, computers, other IT equipment (networks and phones), new medical technologies, and new medicines have allowed increased economic output to grow without any limits. The new pollution control methods in developed economies have helped reduce pollution in water and air, and progress has been made toward achieving sustainable environmental performance. Alternate energy resources are being explored in the form of solar, wind, nuclear, and hydrogen. It seems as long as new technologies continue to emerge, new products will continue to make their way into the markets, and consumers will buy them, allowing economic output to grow. The shrinking population in some countries is not able to benefit from this growth. As a result, the overall growth rate of these economies is either flat or insignificant.

The important question is if this incessant growth has any limitation due to the deteriorating environment (global warming) or some other natural resource limitation. Again, it seems human beings, due to their inquisitiveness, boldness, and enterprising nature will continue to find ways to grow and, at the same time, manage environmental concerns (e.g., COP-27 conference in Sharm El-Sheikh, Egypt is an attempt in this direction). If this holds true, labour productivity will continue to grow. If it is so, then the size of the workforce will be the key factor influencing the growth of the real GDP. It means for countries, which are experiencing a shrinking workforce, a possible solution is to encourage its current population to grow its workforce (provide an incentive to have children) and simultaneously encourage legal immigration of skilled and educated workforce.

Immigration has been a political and social issue in many countries, especially over the last few years. Yes, illegal immigration must be stopped, or it will create law and order problems in the new country. From an economic growth point of view, legal immigration may help grow the GDP. Immigration of a skilled and educated workforce may be a big plus for these countries with a shrinking population, and through this policy, they will be able to push the growth of their GDPs. Still, social aspects of the growing immigrant population may cause uneasiness in some of the native population. Locals may think their jobs are taken away by skilled and less expensive immigrants, causing social unrest and emotional biases against legal immigrants. Though, US immigration policy in the twentieth century has helped the US tremendously gain an edge over other countries in innovation (e.g., R&D) and development of new technologies, immigration issues must be handled carefully (by taking good care of those who are displaced to other jobs due to immigration). These displaced workers must get appropriate training and placement help to find other opportunities based on their own comparative advantage.

Thus, in summary, the growth of real GDP can be sustained or enhanced by improving labour productivity and increasing the size of the workforce. Labour productivity can be increased by savings and investing in physical capital and human capital. It means we must invest in the training and education of people. We must invest in R&D and new technologies. We must encourage entrepreneurship. Also, we must invest in the site's infrastructure, build and maintain good transportation modes (roads, bridges, and rail and sea transportation). The growth, though, must respect the sustainability of our natural resources and environment and help reduce global warming by achieving net zero carbon emissions. Finally, we must grow our workforce size appropriately and sensibly, by respecting local social issues.

5.2 Understand Comparative and Absolute Advantages of Countries, Businesses and Individuals – Take Advantage of the Knowledge and Concept

We have often observed how businesses in developed economies based on old methods and technologies or that require cheap labour move to developing economies. This phenomenon can be explained by using the comparative advantage approach.

According to comparative advantage theory, countries' business competence can be explained based on their absolute advantage and comparative advantage in producing different goods and services. For example, country A produces 200 light bulbs or 80 cotton shirts in a given period. Country B on the other hand produces 100 light bulbs or 200 cotton shirts in that given time. Suppose, country A needs 100 light bulbs and 40 cotton shirts while country B needs 50 light bulbs and 100 cotton shirts. We see country A has the absolute advantage in producing light bulbs while country B has the absolute advantage in producing cotton shirts. Country A's opportunity cost is 2.5 light bulbs for each cotton shirt (or vice versa, 1 light bulb will cost 0.4 per cotton shirt). While Country B's opportunity cost is 0.5 light bulbs for each cotton shirt. It means if country A chooses to make one cotton shirt it has to sacrifice 2.5 light bulbs. In the same way, country B will have to sacrifice 0.5 light bulbs if it chooses to make one additional shirt. What we have to sacrifice to accomplish something else is what we call opportunity cost. Country A's opportunity cost to produce a shirt is 2.5 light bulbs, while country B's opportunity cost to produce a shirt is 0.5 light bulbs. At this point, we can introduce the concept of comparative advantage. We can say the comparative advantage of country A is to produce light bulbs as its opportunity cost is lower than country B's to accomplish the same goal. Country B's comparative advantage is to produce cotton shirts. In this way, if country A just produces light bulbs while country B produces cotton shirts, the overall productivity of the two countries will be higher than if they both produce both items. In an hour, the maximum combined production of both countries would be 200 light bulbs and 200 cotton shirts. While if they both produce both things, they together will produce 150 light bulbs and 140 cotton shirts and meet the needed demand for these items. It is clear from the above example that when countries specialize in certain work areas based on their comparative advantages, they together produce the most items or they have to work less to meet the demands of these countries.

The important message based on this theory is that even if a country has an absolute advantage to produce a product over other countries, the comparative advantage differences allow countries to exchange products resulting in an economic pie growing bigger. The likely impact of this theory is as economies get matured, their focus becomes goods and services that are based on higher skills and high technology. Low-tech products, labour intense manufacturing will become more expensive in these markets (opportunity cost will be high in these countries to produce these products while developing economies will have a comparative advantage over matured economies to produce these results). The overall impact of these changes is that slowly these labour-intensive, low-tech products move from developed economies to developing economies. At times this causes political and social challenges when industries start moving from one country to the other based on comparative advantages. Several examples of this scenario include the transfer of textiles, cement manufacturing, and other low-tech manufacturing from matured economies to developing economies (including some low-tech services also such as calling centers transfer from the US to India, and other countries).

Globalisation has caused a big impact on changing the world's economic landscape. The developing economies have had sustained growth of 7-8 percent. Due to advancements in technology, international trade has become much cheaper. As a result, developing economies are becoming more competitive in areas in which developed economies used to dominate. Forces of comparative advantage are shifting lower value-added components of manufacturing and services from developed to developing economies. These forces are now resulting in significant changes in the employment structure of the US economy. As such not much growth has been realised in the manufacturing, engineering, and consulting sector of the economy in the last 20 years (these components of the economy are called the trade-able sector of the economy. Most growth in the last 20 years in the US has come from the non-tradable sector of the economy and that includes healthcare, government, hotel and restaurant, and construction industries. It means changing comparative forces are creating a new landscape worldwide, forcing jobs to move from one region to the other region of the globe. Considering the fast-changing technological advancement and as a result economies, the US must move faster to maintain its current comparative advantage in the high-tech sector, health area, and green energy sector of the economy. For this to happen, the US must focus on having a world-class education system (including world-class trade and community colleges), enhance forces on research and development, encourage entrepreneurship and provide incentives to those who help implement these initiatives, and ultimately commercialise new higher values added products and services.

Managers must be aware of these market factors/ forces to determine or have some idea of the life cycle of products in matured markets. As technology improves, low-tech jobs will always move to develop or less mature economies because their opportunity costs are lower to handle these jobs. Matured economies due to these market factors or forces are forced to focus on high-tech goods and services because their opportunity cost is lower if they do so. They have a comparative advantage for high-tech jobs.

This idea of comparative advantage is useful in businesses and our daily work lives also. The comparative advantage theory supports specialisation of expertise by these companies. At work, when we assign jobs to our team members we must do so by taking care of comparative advantage of each team member rather than their absolute advantage. It is very tempting to assign a task or project to someone who has an absolute advantage over other team members for the work at hand. Nonetheless, we should think if the person has a comparative advantage and also consider what will be sacrificed if this person is assigned to a particular task. This is what the opportunity cost is for using this person for the task at hand. Other team members may not be as good as the previous member is for the task but the opportunity cost for using the second person may be much lower than for the previous member, justifying the decision that we use the second person for the job even if this person ranks lower in absolute advantage for this job than other team members. The second person will rank highest though in comparative advantage, and therefore this person should be assigned to do the job at hand. Also many times, the question comes to using contractors versus our own workforce to do a certain task. Again, the decision should be based on comparative advantage and opportunity cost. If our own employees can do some other higher value-added task in the same amount of time, the decision could be to continue to use the contractor to work for the lower-value-added task.

5.2 Key Indicators of Economy Health

Businesses perform well when the economy of the region or country is growing. On the other hand, if the country's economy is not good (slow or in recession), businesses will suffer and not make as much profit. Depending on the health of the economy, businesses may have to change their strategies for the launch of new products, business expansion, and merger and acquisition. In tough economic times, it may be very difficult to stay profitable for many companies. If the debt is too high, it may be very challenging for these companies to pay off their debt and meet their obligations on interest payments. In a growing economy, businesses must be ready to grow. Hence, it is very important for business managers to be watchful of the health of the economy and know about the key indicators of the economy.

What are the key indicators of the health of an economy? Broadly speaking, economic indicators can be divided into three categories. These are leading, coincidental, and lagging indicators. Leading indicators of the economy are those that change before the economy changes. Coincidental indicators are those that move with the economy. Lagging indicators are those that do not change with the economy until a few quarters of the economy have passed.

Here is a summary of some of these key indicators (note that any of these indicators should not be considered in isolation; rather, a group of indicators should be considered to assess the overall health of the economy).

Leading Indicators: Consumer Confidence Index (CCI)

The US CCI is a leading indicator. It measures consumer

confidence in the economy. It is expressed in percentage and set at one hundred for the year 1985. Opinions on the current conditions of the economy make up 40 percent of the index, while expectations of future economic conditions count for 60 percent. A total of 5,000 households are included in the summary. The Federal Reserve considers the CCI in making its decision on interest rate changes.

Housing Starts

New housing starts and new building permits are other indicator of economic growth. A trend in this indicator or year-to-year comparison can be an indicator of economic health.

US S&P Case-Shiller Home Price Index

Real estate prices are a big driver of credit availability in the economy. The S&P Case-Shiller 20-City Composite Home Price Index measures changes in residential house prices in twenty metropolitan regions in the US. The base year for this index is 2000 at level 100. In January 2015, this index was reported to be 173.4. Before the mortgage crisis and market crisis in 2006, this index had achieved a high of 206. As of this writing (July 2022), the index is close to three hundred. This index is reported monthly.

If this index is too high, it may be a sign of overheating economy or a bubble in the economy, as in 2006. Mortgages and loans secured by the real estate market are major risk areas for banks. If real estate prices start falling, banks become conservative and will hold higher reserves to cover any losses due to defaults. On the other hand, if real estate prices increase quite a bit, the banks tend to lend more money as the collateral will be worth more than the load. However, this lending tendency and temptation of more and more profit by lending funds in the rising mortgage market may create a bubble in the market. This is a dangerous sign for the economy. The US S&P Case-Shiller Index is, thus, a useful indicator to assess the health of the economy.

Purchasing Managers Index (PMI)

PMI is an important indicator for US manufacturing and the US economy. This indicator is estimated based on surveys of more than four hundred purchasing managers in the US. The indicator is based on the weighted average of sub-indicators, including production level, new orders, supplier deliveries (if they are coming faster or slower), inventories (growing or shrinking), and employment level. A reading of a PMI of fifty indicates that the economy is expanding. It is a leading indicator for future GDP. If PMI is below forty-two, the economy may be falling into recession. In June 2022, the PMI was fifty-three.

JP Morgan Global Plant Manufacturing Index

This index measures factory activity or output globally on a monthly basis. A score of fifty is considered neutral (no change in output over the previous month).

Consumer Credit

This indicator is a leading indicator of economic health in the US. An increase can be a leading indicator that the economy is set to grow more rapidly.

Jobless Claims

This report is published weekly. This weekly data can be quite fluctuating due to its short-term averaging period. Rather, economy or market analysts use a four-month moving average of jobless claims data.

Stock Market

The stock market is generally a leading indicator of the economy. The stock market will decline first before the economy declines. On the other hand, the stock market will improve first before the sustained improvement in the economy. However, sometimes due to external interventions such as the current US federal bond-buying back programme and infusing higher liquidity in the market, the stock market may improve, but the real economy of the country may still be weak (e.g., during COVID-19 in 2020-21, the US increased the market liquidity greatly by providing cash to people and businesses. The stock market did well during these two years, though, it was not a good indicator of the real health of the US economy). Similarly, the Dow Jones index in early 2008 was at its peak, and most experts were confirming that the economy was healthy and would continue to be healthy.

The US stock market crashed in Sept. 2008, forcing the US economy and the world economy into recession. The artificial interventions in the market before this crash created an economic bubble. Easy availability of mortgages under the re-strengthened *Community Reinvestment Act* of the nineties to low-income as well as middle class encouraged people to secure easy loans without requiring them to document their incomes and assets and build and buy new and expensive homes. These purchases, otherwise, would be out of their reach in normal lending practices. Fannie Mae and Freddie Mac had to repurchase the mortgage loans that third parties had written to low-income and other urban people. These bad loans had to be written off (this was referred to as the subprime crisis). Many banks failed due to this crisis. However, the Federal Reserve had to rescue some big banks by using tax payer's money.

The lesson is that other indicators, along with stock market movement, must be looked at to assess the real economic health of the country. Certainly, improving the stock market instills confidence in the masses, and this helps stimulate the economy. However, artificial simulators may go too far out of line and create a false sense of improving the economy.

Bond Market

The bond market is an important leading indicator for the economic activity of the future. A bond value is the present value of all future cash flows at a discount rate. A bond yield is the discount rate that makes the present value of the bond's future cash flows equal to its price. Short-term interest rates are set by the nation's central banks. Long-term interest rates, on the other hand, are set by the market. It is really the reaction of the bond market to future economic activity. If the bond prices are high, meaning bond yields are low, it means future inflation will be low. If bond yields, on the other hand, are high (as they are soaring in the current year 2022), it means economic activity is expected to increase, increasing inflation and interest rate (and lowering bond prices).

Stock Market Volatility Index (VIX)

This index is a key measure of market volatility and investor sentiment for the next thirty days. The index is a measure of market risk and is also referred to as an "investor's fear gauge." VIX values greater than thirty are generally associated with a large amount of volatility, while values below twenty generally correspond to a less stressful time. VIX was 23.9 in November of 2022 (according to the US Federal Reserve), indicating a relative calmness in the market (this index was almost 29 in June 2022).

Coincidental Indicators

Gross Domestic Product (GDP)

GDP is the most recognised indicator for assessing a nation's economic health and discussed in Section 3.1.

Gross National Product (GNP)

GNP also comprises the total production of a nation, but it excludes the earnings of foreigners on its land and includes the amount earned by its people in other nations other than its own.

Balance of Payment

The balance of payment is the summary of economic transactions that occur between the residents of a country with another country.

Consumer Price Index (CPI)

Consumer price index is another indicator of the economic health of a country. CPI is an indicator of inflation. It's used in adjusting the amounts of salaries, wages, and pensions in light of inflation. An increase in inflation or even the expectations of higher inflation can be enough for banks to increase rates on savings accounts, CDs, and money market accounts. Current mortgage rates typically move higher as the prospect for long-term economic growth or inflation increases. This index has increased 7.7 percent for last 12 months, ending October 2022.

Retail Sales

This is a coincidental indicator. The sales data covers the prior month's sales. The sales data used in the survey are from all-size companies as well as multinational companies and small-town companies. It is considered a pre-inflationary indicator and is of much interest to investors. The Federal Reserve takes this data into consideration in making its decision on interest rates. If during a normal business cycle, there is a sharp increase in retail sales, this may be an indicator of a growing economy.

Federal Spending and Debt

These are coincidental economic indicators. Both federal spending and debt rise during a recession as the government tries to stimulate the economy by increasing spending. However, if the federal spending is on unproductive items and debt is too high (that most government revenue is being spent on paying interest on debt), the rising spending and debt may not bode well for the future economy of the country.

Interest Rate, Inflation, and Bond Yield

Interest rates and inflation are coincidental economic indicators. Rising interest rates and inflation signal a slowing economy ahead and, at times, may signal a current overheating (if rising too fast) economy. Bond yield is also a coincidental but counter-cyclic indicator (it means yields tend to fall when the economy improves).

Lagging Indicators

Unemployment Rate

This gives the percentage of the labour force that is capable of working but is presently out of work due to a lack of opportunities. It is an untapped talent of a nation. An increase in this indicator is not a good sign for economic growth. This indicator is a lagging indicator as it keeps rising for two to three months even after the economy starts to improve.

Product Price Index (PPI)

A PPI is a measure of the average price changes received by domestic producers of their output. This index includes all the physical goods-producing industries that make up the US economy (imports are not included). This index is measured on a monthly basis.

Industrial Production Index (IPI)

Industrial production index is another economic indicator that measures the production output of manufacturing, mining, and utilities. It is published monthly by the US Federal Reserve Board. The reference year for this indicator is set at one hundred in the year 2002. If the IPI is increasing month after month, it is a strong sign of a growing economy (or vice versa).

Capacity Utilisation Index

Capacity utilisation index is the ratio between actual production and potential output. If the capacity utilisation of a country is growing, this is a sign of a growing economy. In a slowing economy, the demand for products will reduce, and as a result, capacity utilisation will decrease. Generally, an 82 percent - 85 percent percent capacity utilisation index is a sign of a healthy economy. If this index is over 85 percent, the economy is at risk for high inflation (it means the economy is growing too fast). From April to May 2022, the US capacity utilisation is hovering around 80.8–80.9 percent.

Country Currency Strength

A stable currency signals the sound economic health of the country. A falling currency rate, however, signals weakness in the economy (it means demand for the currency is slowing). A weak currency, though, will favour the export from the country. However, the import will be more expensive. China is accused of artificially keeping its currency weak in order to stay competitive in the global market for its products.

Important Indicators to Indicate if the Market or the Economy Has a Big Bubble That Can Burst Anytime

Most above indicators will individually signal if the market is moving in the right direction or stable or may face some downward pressure. These indicators must be considered collectively to have a fair understanding of the economy and the market. The challenge, though, remains as some indicators will signal in one direction while others may tell a different story, and thus, knowing the real health of the market or economy still remains challenging. The biggest concern is if the market seems to be healthy based on stock market valuation and other indicators if the market will continue to trend up, signaling good health of the overall economy. Or there is a limit, and the healthy market may be due for a crash or big correction. These sudden changes in the market and the economy may catch companies unguarded and prove irreversibly expensive in some cases. Hence, it is very important for business leaders to familiarise themselves with market or economy valuation tools so they have a better appreciation for the economy and the market and can strategise their business plans and executions with better awareness of these external events.

The following two indicators are considered the most important valuation tools to assess if the market may be due for a significant correction or, on the contrary, if the market is way undervalued and must trend up.

1. Robert Shiller's Cyclically Adjusted Price Earnings (CAPE) Ratio

CAPE is another important, widely popular measure for market valuation. CAPE is calculated by taking the S&P 500 price and dividing it by the average of the last ten years of earnings. If the ratio is above the long-term average of around 16 percent, the market is considered expensive (or it is an indication that the economy is heating up). If the CAPE ratio is above twenty-six, the market is considered to be quite vulnerable and has a high possibility of crash or correction (bad news). Or one can say the economy has overheated quite a bit and created a bubble that may burst anytime.

The purpose of ten years averaging is to control business cycle effects. This is a better measurement of market valuation. In November 2022, the CAPE ratio is 27.2 (which was 38.6 a year ago), which is 64 percent higher than the historical means of 16.6. Based on this ratio, the market is quite overvalued currently and has a high possibility of correction.

2. Total Market Cap (TMC) over GDP (Buffett Indicator)

According to Warren Buffett, total market cap to GNP (Gross National Product) is "probably the best single measure of where the valuations stand at any given time." GDP is the total market value of goods and services produced within the boundary of a country by its own residents. GNP is the total market value of goods and services produced by the residents of a country, even if they are living abroad. Historically, GDP and GNP have been within 1 percent of each other. We will use GDP for our further discussion.

As of November 2022, TMC to GDP ratio is around 139.6 percent. This is how the market valuation is done using this ratio:

Total Market Cap / GDP < 50% -------------------> Significantly undervalued

75 < Total Market Cap / GDP < 90% -------- Fair valued

Ratio > 115% ------------ Significantly overvalued

In the year 2000, this ratio was 148 percent while before 2007 crash, this index was higher than 115 percent. In November 2022, the current TMC to GDP ratio is 139.6, while this ratio was close to 190 percent a year ago (note that he US stock market dropped close to 20 percent in 2022). This indicator is still way above 115 percent, and therefore the market, as of November 2022, stays in a significantly overvalued category. This valuation of the market against the GDP indicates that the economy is heading for a significant correction in the near future unless the economy cools down at a good pace soon.

(a) Exchange Rates—Key Economic Influencers

Foreign exchange rates are influenced by many factors, including the economic health of the country, political stability, social stability, and general mood (expectations) of the public for the future. Also, how economic, political, and social conditions are in other countries relatively also influence the exchange rates of currencies. The economic health of a country is generally measured by its GDP growth rate, its public debt, current account deficit (export minus import), inflation rate, and interest rate. Political stability and social stability in a country influence foreign investment and expectation for return on investment based on the perceived risks due to these two factors. Political disturbance or social instability will deter foreign investors and negatively impact the country's currency. If the public is excited about its country's future, this will spur spending, consumption, and economic growth. This kind of public mood will positively help the country's currency. High public debt relative to GDP will be a concern for foreign investors and may depreciate currency value. A decade or so ago, in several European countries, government debts become so high relative to their GDPs that their currencies suffered a great deal (e.g., Spain and Greece). Argentina's currency also had suffered due to its high debt relative to its GDP. Sri Lanka defaulted on foreign debt in 2022 due to not having enough foreign exchange to meet its obligations. Due to the economic challenges the country was experiencing, Sri Lanka rupee plummeted against dollar in the first half of 2022. Global economic slowdown of 2022 has negatively impacted Bangladesh's foreign reserves and in November 2022 the International Monetary Fund (IMF) provided a $4.5 billion rescue package to the country so it can meet its foreign debt obligation (the World Bank had called Bangladesh an inspiring story of growth. www.npr.org, Nov 9 2022). As a result, the currency of Bangladesh taka suffered greatly against the US dollar in 2022.

The economic health of a country is reflected in the country's inflation and the interest rate it offers to investors. Thus, prevailing inflation and interest rate in countries are the two most important factors influencing the exchange rates. More specifically, the inflation rate differential and interest rate differential between two countries influence its exchange rate most (assuming political and social factors in both countries are stable and so do not influence currencies significantly). Let's now discuss inflation and interest rate differentials and their impacts on exchange rates (References: 1. How Does Inflation Affect the Exchange Rates between Two Nations. www.investopedia.com. Investopedia Team, March 07, 2022. 2. Foreign Exchange and the Dollar, Chapter 19, pages 511-522, Macroeconomics, Second Edition, Michael Perkins,)

Inflation Rate Differentials

Let's assume the inflation rate in country A is 6 percent while in country B is 2 percent. It means the purchasing power of country A's currency will depreciate by 6 percent annually while the purchasing power of the currency of country B will depreciate by 2 percent. This inflation differential of 4 percent will make country B's currency more powerful relative to the currency of country A. Assuming all other factors are relatively unchanged (interest rates and political and economic factors) in these two countries, the exchange rate will also change according to the inflation differential (4 percent change in the inflation differential means roughly a 4 percent change in the exchange rate theoretically). However, the real-world situation is not this simple. To control inflation, the country's central bank will regulate and change the interest rate. What impact this likely change in interest rate in the two countries will have on the exchange rate is discussed in the next section.

Interest Rate Differentials

From a highly simplistic point of view, higher interest rates erode currency values. This is because countries (their central banks) use the interest rate to control inflation. However, it is not the absolute interest rate that impacts the country's currency value; rather, it is the "real" interest rate that impacts the country's currency. The real interest rate is the difference between the interest rate and the inflation rate. Hence, the level of real interest rates in countries will influence their currencies relative to each other. A high-interest rate as such will attract foreign investment, influencing currency positively. On the other hand, a high-interest rate will suppress business investment and domestic spending, negatively impacting currency. A low-interest rate will have a reverse impact of a high-interest rate. Real interest rate takes into account inflation. Thus, it is the real interest rates of countries that influence exchange rates the most. Interest rate theory predicts that real interest rates across boundaries will tend to reach equilibrium. It means currencies with higher interest rates will tend to weaken eventually. In the short term, it may not be so due to market and political distortions. In the long run, though, market forces will prevail, and equilibrium will reach for variables). Let's take an example to understand this point a bit more clearly. If in my own country the interest rate is two percent while in the neighboring country, it is five percent, I can deposit my money in the neighbouring country and earn three percent additional interest. If the exchange rate does not change due to this interest rate differential, I will earn an extra interest rate, grow my money faster in the neighbouring country, withdraw it when I need it, and bring it back to my own country. However, the real interest rate across countries will reach equilibrium, and as a result, the country with a higher interest rate (and a higher real interest rate) will experience a weakening currency. It means though I have earned extra interest on my money in the neighbouring country, I will lose this gain when I convert my money back from local currency to my currency.

Purchasing Power Parity

Purchasing power parity (PPP) captures the overall impact of inflation, interest, and the overall health of a country's economy on the country's currency. Purchasing power parity means the equal value of money in different countries. It means in an ideal world, a basket of goods should cost the same in all countries of the world (the inherent value of the basket is the same in all countries, and so different currencies should have equal purchasing power once they are adjusted for exchange rates). Let's take an example. If this basket of goods (representing the entire economy of a country) costs $5 in the US and Rs. 500 in India, at the current (July 2022) exchange rate of Rs. 79 for a dollar, the basket will cost $6.33 in India. It means it is costlier in India. However, the PPP theory says that money should have equal value (purchasing power) in different countries. This disparity in the current exchange rate then indicates that the rupee is likely to become weaker in the future and ideally may be trading at Rs 100 for a dollar (then our basket will cost $5 in India also). As there could be many factors (GDP expected future growth rate, debt level, current-account deficit, and political and social stabilities) that will have an influence on the exchange rate, the PPP should be considered a useful tool to indicate how a currency can move directionally against the other currency.

The Big Mac index is used to assess how directionally exchange rates may change. This index is published by the British magazine the *Economist*. McDonald's sets Big Mac rates in different countries considering local economic factors (prices of items that are purchased locally to make Big Mac). The Big Mac index is used to teach the impact of PPP on the exchange rates of currencies. It is not an official governmental tool that is used to assess how currencies may move against each other. Nonetheless, it is a powerful teaching tool to assess how PPPs of currencies are likely to impact exchange rates.

5.3 Market Concentration

As business leaders and facility managers, we must know how

competitive our market is for our products. If the market is very competitive, we must pay close attention to pricing, quality of our products, and customer service to differentiate ourselves from our competition. If we are the market leader, we can introduce new products in the market relatively easily. Others will benchmark against us. At the same time, if a firm is a market leader, the firm has the risk of becoming complacent and not being innovative in developing new products in a lack of competition. Business leaders must know that government agencies constantly monitor market concentration closely and the behaviour of firms if the market is not very concentrated.

Generally, marketing and sales will have an idea about the market concentration. To take subjectivity out of the market concentration discussion, I would like to introduce here two popular methods to quantify market concentration. These two methods include (1) the Herfindahl index and (2) the four-firm concentration ratio.

Herfindahl Index (HI)

It is a very popular indicator and is used to measure the sizes of firms in relation to the industry as an indicator of the amount of competition among them. This index is calculated as follows:

$$HI = S1^2 + S2^2 + S3^2 + \ldots + Sn^2$$

Where:

S1 is the market share of Firm 1

Sn is the market share of Firm n.

Based on the above calculations, if

$HI < 0.1$, the industry is considered un-concentrated, and the industry is very competitive

$0.1 < HI < 0.18$, the industry concentration is considered moderate

$HI > 0.18$, the industry is highly concentrated.

Let's take an example. If the top five firms in an industry have the following market share:

S1 = 20%, S2 = 18%, S3 = 12%, S4 = 10%, S5 = 6%, and the remaining 10 firms have 3% each,

$HI = (0.2)^2 + (0.18)^2 + (0.12)^2 + (0.1)^2 + (0.06)^2 + 10\,(0.03)^2 = 0.11$

It means this industry is moderately concentrated. Note that the HI includes the market share of every firm in the industry.

Four-firm concentration ratio

In this method, the sum of the percent market shares of the four largest firms in the industry is estimated. The market concentration of these firms is classified as follows:

- Monopoly: if the sum is close to 100 percent
- Oligopoly (small number of firms only): if the sum is greater than 40 percent
- Oligopoly to perfect competition: if the sum is less than 40 percent
- Perfect competition: if the sum is very low

For the same firms that were used to calculate HI, the four-firm concentration ratio would be 60 percent, which classifies this industry as an oligopoly market. Also, the HI method provides a complete picture of the industry than the four-firm concentration method.

6

Strive to Go beyond Operational Excellence for Long-Term Survivability

Leaders and managers must take it to heart that just operational excellence is not a guarantee to survival or to ensure the leadership position of their company in their respective industry. First, let's closely examine what exactly operational excellence means by defining each term separately.

An operation consists of employees, customers, community, and various business processes related to the operation, engineering, quality, raw material management, finance, and purchasing. Suppliers and government are also key entities involved in any operation. An operation is also concerned about its environmental impact, the types of machines used, the health and safety of employees, vendor management, and its corporate social responsibility. Thus, an operation could be a very complex entity. Unless various processes or entities within the organisations are managed and optimised carefully, any operation will have inefficiencies that will make the entire operation less effective and productive.

Now let's examine excellence and what it means. Excellence means being extremely good at what we are doing. It does not mean we are perfect. It means that we are so good that others look up to us and want to learn from us.

Operational excellence then means to be really good (outstanding) in running our operation and be in the top tier. Simply put, it means no entity can run their business better than us. This means we understand what value drivers and cost drivers are out there to maximise value creation. In operational excellence, cost owners are empowered to drive the cost down by improving efficiencies and eliminating waste (e.g., using lean manufacturing concepts and prioritizing). We understand what our customers want. We have a loyal customer following. We know what things must be fixed in our business to get better. We have a good understanding of our business, and we can prioritise and fix those things first that will maximise value creation.

Operational excellence aims to maximise output for the same input by optimizing various processes based on the priority of the organisation. In operational excellence, we don't strive for excellence for each process. Rather we strive for excellence for the entire organisation collectively. It means our goal is to maximise output for the given raw material (input) without compromising on government requirements. In operational excellence, we eliminate waste by maximizing output and minimizing waste (or minimizing input), and as a result, we aim to maximise the margin of the business.

Operational excellence is not a target, but rather, it is a journey. On this journey, we prioritise our goals based on what processes we decide to fix first. We identify actions based on our goals and execute these actions to accomplish our goals. Operational excellence encourages data collection and data analysis. Accurate data and related trend analysis provide important insight into the business and helps identify opportunities to capture. Once the identified goals are achieved, we go back, review our processes, prioritise, and optimise our processes again by achieving new goals. Thus, the journey continues. It is a continuous improvement process. In the manufacturing environment, operational excellence inspires lean manufacturing. It means key processes are optimised for effectiveness and efficiency.

Operational excellence inspires flawless execution of business strategy and identified plans. This means that we stay focused on short-term goals. Also, organisational excellence is a part of the operational excellence journey. A right organisation with the right people in the right places is very important to be successful in our operational excellence journey. We must engage and inspire our workforce to be successful in our operational excellence journey.

Though operational excellence is very helpful in making the business stronger, a real concern nonetheless remains, and that is if operational excellence is enough and will prepare the business for long-term success. Before we answer this question, let's talk about concepts of creative destruction.

The idea of creative destruction was coined by the Austrian economist Joseph Schumpeter in his *Capitalism, Socialism and Democracy* in 1942. He described creative destruction as a process that continuously revolutionises the economic structure from within, incessantly destroying the old one and creating a new one in its place. It means old ways of doing business with old technologies are replaced with new ways and new technologies. Creative destruction in the market is the equivalent of natural destruction in nature caused by imbalances in the ecosystem. Floods, fires, landslides, or tsunamis cause unprecedented destruction in the ecosystem. Nonetheless, the ecosystem is remarkably resilient and agile and will accommodate disruptive changes caused by natural disasters and emerge stronger. For example, forest fires can be a form of creative destruction (David K. Hurst, blog on Facebook, February 6, 2021). Fires cause openings in the forest canopy to open up so sunlight can reach smaller plants. This disruptive change stimulates ecosystem diversity. The burning of trees enriches the soil with calcium, potassium, phosphorus, and other minerals. External factors such as carbon dioxide and methane introduced by man-made activities also destroy the balance of the ecosystem and accelerate creative destruction. These ecological systems are better positioned for adaptation when they are diverse, populated with species, and more tolerant to post-disturbance environments (S. Buma and C. Schultz, "Disturbances as Opportunities," *Journal of Applied Ecology*, February 7, 2020). It is interesting to note that financial markets act more like complex ecosystems with different species that are competing, evolving, innovating, and adapting (Briar Eastwood, MIT Management, April 26, 2007). Financial markets are also highly competitive and innovative due to people being highly driven, creative, emotional, rational as well as irrational at times.

An example of creative destruction is the evolution of PCs and the death of mainframe computers as a result. This disruption resulted in the creation of a new PC industry altogether. Some other examples are as follows. Internal engine combustion replaced horse-driven wagons and the way of transportation. Internal combustion engines caused the birth of the automobile industry and the aviation industry. Railroads came into being as a result of steam engines. Later on, long-haul trucks replaced rail transportation a great deal. In the United States, the agriculture industry employed 40 percent of the population in the early twentieth century to produce food for 90 million people. At the end of the century, only 2 percent of the population was actively engaged in agriculture to produce food for more than 300 million people. This revolution in the agricultural industry happened due to an increase in productivity as a result of new farming methods and technologies. More recently, the internet caused the creative destruction of many jobs, including retail clerks, bank tellers, travel agents, and office secretaries, and created new jobs for programmemers, mapmakers, and online shopping. Fax and typewriters were replaced by emailing, texting, and computer word processors. New online industries emerged, such as Amazon, Uber, e-Bay, and Airbnb. The telephone industry also went through the process of creative destruction. Several hundred thousand jobs in the telephone industry were destroyed due to the emergence of mobile phones and smartphones. In developed countries, labour-intensive jobs in mining and manufacturing were replaced by higher-paying service industry jobs.

Creative destruction is mainly caused by disruptive technologies. Incremental innovation, such as improvement in machine efficiency or labour productivity, or quality improvements, does not cause creative destruction. This is because these routine innovations do not result in new industries. Creative destruction is caused because businesses are expected to improve constantly and meet various conflicting expectations. For example, consumers want lower costs, suppliers want higher prices for their raw materials, owners want higher profits, the public expects lower environmental impacts, and government regulations require compliance with stringent standards. These higher and conflicting expectations inspire entrepreneurs for new technologies and a new way of doing business. As a result, disruptive technologies appear on the scene and cause creative destruction by replacing old technologies. Businesses that are focused just on operational excellence and do not pay much attention to innovation are caught unguarded by disruptive technologies. The problem for such businesses is that in the beginning, while new technologies are in their infancy and are not very effective and profitable, these businesses don't pay attention to these technologies. They, on their own, don't reallocate resources to innovation as they have to meet their short-term profitability and cash goals. Once their profit starts eroding as a result of new market entrants with new technologies, the existing businesses find themselves in a downward spiral as their eroding profits do not allow them to reallocate resources to emerging technologies anymore. As a result, they risk their future to disruptive technologies.

Due to the reality of creative destruction in the market, existing corporations risk their survival if they simply rely on regular adjustments and improvements caused by operational excellence. Leaders and managers must consider the concept of operational excellence as an insufficient tool for a corporation seeking to evolve at the pace and scale of the markets. Corporate leaders and managers must have the energy and time to recognise and manage the process of creative destruction. Short-term goals set for managers and leaders are, as such, contrary to the long-term goals of maximizing the company's value. To sustain a long-term leadership role, the company must blend innovation with operational excellence. In fact, with innovation, the company can trigger the creative destruction of its own ineffective or inefficient methods, products, or technology. Creative destruction is overall a good thing for the industry, market, and society. Yes, this process can eliminate inefficiency or firms that have not been forward-looking and were not prepared for step-changes caused by creative destruction. After creative destruction has happened, the market is way better off now with new excitement (energy), as customers benefit from improved and cost-effective choices. The root cause of creative destruction is not continuous improvement but rather disruptive changes in the market due to groundbreaking innovations. A well-run company, with a focus on operational excellence, could be a victim of creative destruction, unless the company has prepared itself in advance for any disruptive changes caused by innovation. In addition, the business must be resilient and agile enough to adapt to any sudden changes in the market. Hence, a blend of operational excellence and innovation is the key to the long-term success of businesses.

7

Additional Know-How for Manufacturing Leaders

In the previous chapters, we talked about sustainable development, the basics of finances, leadership, and motivational tips. Those tips apply to all settings, manufacturing, and nonmanufacturing. In manufacturing, leaders are faced with several other challenges. I believe manufacturing leaders and managers will find the following tips useful and their teams and sites will benefit once they apply them.

7.1 Choose Your Team Carefully

As a manager, you will have an ambitious agenda to implement to create value for stakeholders. You will do it through your team of managers and other leaders of the organisation. We would like to infuse energy into the team so the team can be mobilised and turn the organisation can be mobilised. It is always good to have team members from diverse backgrounds with open minds. We need team members who believe in change and are willing to take an intelligent risk. We need those on our team who have a great attitude towards work and life. We would like to have those who believe in the organisation's vision. If we accept team members who do not have energy, do not believe in change, and do not have a positive attitude, these people will fail us and the organisation. At times it could happen that some of these people will have a great experience and have institutional knowledge, but they will not join us fully in our mission to bring about needed change. They will find reasons not to try new things. They will give us reasons repeatedly why certain things will not work (and that they tried these things long ago). They will not volunteer information unless asked specifically. Watch them. Do they actively participate in meetings and make a positive contribution to intimidate other team players? If you have team members with these characteristics, you as a leader must take immediate action and consider removing them from the group or organisation. Yes, we can assess if they fit somewhere else in the organisation based on their comparative advantage. Should they be allowed to improve their performance? The problem with this approach is it is a fast-moving world, we also move fast, or else we are left behind. Because of their lack of support for the team and your efforts to make drastic changes, your efforts to change as fast will be wasted. The entire team will be discouraged if we accepted their bad behaviours. We risk losing some good, talented people from our team if we have not removed those who are not supporting the team, organisation goals, and vision. The momentum you would like to build will not be achieved with people with poor attitudes on our team. The risk is way too high to coach people in leadership positions with bad attitudes, negative energy, and unwillingness to change. If someone is lacking a skill but has good values and virtues, this person can be mentored and coached successfully. People lacking good values and virtues will very likely waste our time and efforts if we think we can change them and make them good performers who will support our vision, and organisational goals, support the team and move fast enough. With these factors in mind, if we think a certain person can be coached successfully and may be considered for a different position in the same location or different location, a decision should be made quickly so your current efforts to bring about necessary changes will not continue to suffer.

Once we have built our team. We are ready to infuse efficiency and inspire the organisation to march towards achieving excellence.

Now, we support this team, train them as necessary, coach them, have an open discussion, challenge their ideas and allow them to challenge yours. This is our winning team now.

7.2 Must Have Commitment to EHS

First and foremost, site leaders must make it clear to management team members and other employees that subpar Environment Health and Safety (EHS) is non-negotiable. Full EHS compliance is their license to lead. If they are not engaged in EHS and fail in their environmental and safety responsibilities, they should not hold leadership positions. This means that everyone must take EHS very seriously and any known violations must be dealt with accordingly. Human safety and product safety must never be compromised. Similarly, there must be no compromise at all on environmental compliance. It means each site employee must be committed to 100 percent environmental compliance all the time. Full environmental compliance is our license to operate. So no compromise must be accepted on environmental compliance.

Good businesses and their leaders must go beyond compliance though and aim to minimise their environmental and carbon footprints. Businesses that are sincere about reducing their environmental and carbon footprints will talk about what actions they are taking and also publish their environmental reports on their company's webpage.

7.3 Must Practice Effective Communication and Address Employee's Basic Needs on Priority

In the manufacturing environment, good communication on issues of interest to employees is highly critical. In my extensive experience in manufacturing and other industries employees have rated poor communication by management as one of their top issues of concern. As a result, the workforce is frustrated and disengaged with a net result of low morale and low productivity. Managers and leaders must make sure they have appropriate channels to communicate with employees. The communication must be regular. Core players of the management team must be well versed on issues being talked about and should be able to answer questions by others about the business.

Another important point is to engage employees in a positive way. Also, site leaders must make sure employees' basic concerns are addressed promptly (e.g., break room issues, bathroom not clean, not enough light, and so forth). If the site management is not able to take care of the very basic complaints from employees, the site will not be able to build a strong and engaged team. These are hygiene issues as called by Hertzberg and must be addressed to engage employees meaningfully.

7.4 Make Site Vision and Site Goals Clear to All

As discussed earlier, the site vision must be clear to all employees. The site must set its three to five goals (five max or nobody remembers) for the current year and share them with all employees. Highly engaged employees will be able to tell you site goals if asked. Most employees will be able to cite these goals if the site culture is engaging and motivating to employees. Department goals must support site goals for good alignment. Individual goals must be set in line with the site and department goals. The role and responsibilities of all employees must be defined clearly and shared with concerned employees.

7.5 Have an Effective Performance Review Programme

Furthermore, the site must have an effective performance review process. We recommend performance reviews be done at least twice every year. An employee must know his or her strengths and development opportunities. We must be respectful, yet candid in our feedback. Never belittle a person. We must start with the strengths of the employee. We must acknowledge that there is always room for improvement for everybody (including ourselves). Then, share specific examples where performance could be better. We must know that these reviews are not discipline tools. During these performance reviews, there must never be a surprise to an employee with the feedback if managers and supervisors are keeping in constant contact with each other throughout the year. To assist the development of high performers, individual development plans (IDPs) with specifics (what must be done by when and who will be able to help) could be a great tool to use.

7.6 Implement a Training and Development Programme

Furthermore, site leaders must implement a training and development programme for employees. Leaders must delegate and empower our team members according to their skills, experience, and motivation. For this to happen, we must train our direct reports and prepare them for taking on additional responsibilities. Any new supervisor or manager must be trained in leadership, people skills, and communication issues before being in charge of people. Many times, even star individual performers fail when they are assigned to supervisory roles. We must prepare them for success before giving them independent charge of running a shift or an operation. The best approach is to assign a seasoned mentor to the new supervisor or manager. This will provide insightful tips when dealing with people-related issues.

7.7 Celebrate Your Wins Appropriately

Good leaders and managers must create a culture where employees have appropriate celebrations for better-than-expected results or achieving important milestones. The point is we must create a culture where we work together as a great team, achieve results, and celebrate. We, along with our team, must have fun as well in the journey and so must learn to laugh together. Don't become robots with long faces. Play hard, be passionate, and challenge each other for becoming better yet must have fun in the journey together with your team.

7.7 Use Digital Technology and Take Care of Your Equipment Proactively

In manufacturing, we must take care of not only people but also of the equipment and production processes (batch or continuous process). We have talked much about motivation and leadership in earlier chapters. As we must take good care of people, we must do the same for processes and equipment. First and foremost, we must make sure we use digital technology and IT tools to constantly monitor our processes and equipment. Processes and equipment must be interlocked appropriately to have a reliable operation. If we are not at this stage of using technology in managing our operation, we are already behind and will be outdated in the near future, subjecting us to the peril of creative destruction. The use of the right technology makes our operation more efficient and productive. We stay innovative. Our cost is controlled, making us more competitive. Manufacturing leaders and managers must build a case for the application of IT, digital technology, and automation for their sites. Maintenance of equipment is another key area which must be paid close attention to.

Equipment without care will fail and cost the business dearly. Manufacturing leaders and managers must ensure the site has a good maintenance programme. A maintenance programme is the backbone of a manufacturing facility. Without a good maintenance programme, the site will fail in achieving its results. Hence, leaders and managers must ensure they have a top-class maintenance programme at their site.

As an example, a standard maintenance programme pyramid is provided in the exhibit below. We note from this pyramid as we move up the pyramid and take care of additional elements of the maintenance programme, the programme becomes more robust and reliable (note the colour scheme in the pyramid). A green colour means this block is very solid, and no further action is needed. The yellow colour in the pyramid means the site is working on these blocks and trying to turn them green. The red colour indicates the site is way behind in this area and must have a lot more work to do to turn yellow and then green.

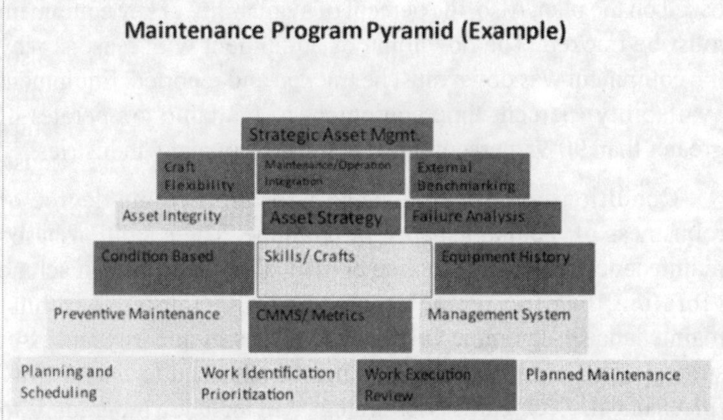

A good maintenance programme consists of a maintenance budget, planning of maintenance work based on work order prioritisation, and work supervision. A reliable computerised management system (CMMS) will be the tool to help manage work orders and preventive maintenance routes and routines. In today's world, if you don't use a good CMMS, the performance of your site, the morale of your maintenance people, and the good upkeep of equipment may be questioned seriously. A good maintenance programme will optimise spare parts inventory and have qualified, trained, and motivated maintenance staff. Facilities can use a separate spare parts inventory management programme to manage their inventory. A reliable maintenance programme will include preventive maintenance as a part of their planned and scheduled activities. A preventive maintenance programme includes walk-by inspections of equipment, a lubrication programme for all motors, fans, gearboxes, and balancing of motors and fans to reduce vibration.

The maintenance programme will track some key performance indicators (KPI) and help assess the health of the maintenance programme. These KPIs may include the percent of completed scheduled preventive maintenance work orders (or hours), the percent of unplanned maintenance work orders (or hours), the value of spare parts inventory, and the percent of training completed based on the plan. Also, the percent of availability of key equipment must be tracked. The downtime of equipment with reasons why the equipment was down must be tracked and reported. Equipment availability (percent time equipment is available to operate) of greater than 90-95 percent must be the goal in many industries.

Condition-based maintenance will improve the degree of robustness of the maintenance programme. The condition-based maintenance will include online or manual monitoring of machine vibration, bearing temperatures, and oil samples. A robust maintenance programme will also include asset integrity and asset strategy. This means all key equipment is checked for its integrity (mechanical, electrical). Asset strategy will include a programme to replace old assets. A failure mode and effect analysis (FMEA) will help identify various failure modes and estimate their probability and overall risk of failure. Based on this analysis and prioritisation of high-risk scenarios, one can identify actions that must be taken to address an identified failure mode scenario at hand. For example, if based on the FMEA of a fan, it is identified that the failure mode of its bearing is a high-risk scenario (risk is the probability of failure times of the business consequence of the failure in terms of business loss times number of times this event may happen in a year). If the probability of bearing failure is 0.3, the consequence of this failure is 3, and the expected number of events in a year is 2, then the risk associated with this failure mode is 1.8. We assign a risk score to other failure modes and prioritise high-risk scenarios to follow and take action. The action could be to monitor the bearing temperature and vibration more frequently and replace it proactively based on some criteria for these readings. Another action could be to ensure this bearing is available in-house for use. If the bearing fails, the part is available for replacement immediately. This action may reduce the consequence score and so the overall risk score.

Maintenance technicians, who are highly skilled not only in one area but in more than one area, make the maintenance team and programme stronger. If a maintenance technician can do mechanical as well as electrical work, this kind of flexibility in skills makes the whole maintenance programme strong. An electrician who can do control programmeming too is highly valuable and makes the maintenance team stronger.

A robust maintenance programme will identify all critical pieces of equipment and have a proactive plan to monitor them, repair them promptly if they go down, and have critical spares on hand to replace damaged parts. Many times, a facility suffers because we did not have a plan for critical equipment, and we ran the equipment until it failed. FMEA analysis can be used to identify these critical pieces of equipment. Some equipment may be obvious to experienced maintenance or operations staff that they are critical. FMEA can validate their observations and identify others by doing a systematic analysis of all processes and equipment by the right people.

Maintenance and operations must work hand in hand to take good care of the operational equipment. Operations can do walk-by inspections and report any unusual symptoms on the equipment (e.g., based on noise, temperature, or vibration).

Benchmarking your maintenance programme with other sites within the company or outside of the industry will make us aware of opportunities to improve our programme further. Another point of caution is the maintenance budget. We must analyse what percent of the full budget (or our sales or production) is being allocated to maintenance (upkeep or equipment and capex to replace old equipment). Site leaders or company leaders can save money and improve EBIT or cash flow by reducing their maintenance budget for sure. However, good leaders and managers must be extremely careful. Ideally, the equipment depreciation should be invested back in regular maintenance and replacement of equipment. If your maintenance budget (including capex) is much lower than this amount constantly for many years, please check if the equipment availability has started hurting and availability is no more what it used to be. Unless we address this matter of low budget sooner, the site may find itself in a state of no return and the equipment performance and site performance may be so poor that large capital expenses will be required to revert this sad situation. A good operation can be driven to bankruptcy, if it is not a common practice to allocate enough on equipment maintenance or replacement.

7.9 Production Must Focus on Productivity and Operation Efficiency

Regarding production processes, we must train our operation staff well so they can optimise these processes for production efficiency. If the maintenance department is responsible for equipment availability, production is responsible for production efficiency and quality yield. Together these three factors give us a very important manufacturing indicator for a process or site. This indicator is termed as OEE (operating equipment effectiveness).

OEE of a production line, is thus defined as:

OEE = Availability (%) x Production efficiency (%) x Quality yield (%)

Where availability % is equipment or line % availability to operate (% timeline or equipment is ready to produce).

Production efficiency (%) is actual production by the equipment or production line divided by design or best-demonstrated production by the equipment or line.

Quality yield (%) is % amount or number of products that are sellable.

Let's take an example to understand OEE calculation further. Let's say a piece of production equipment is available to run 95 percent of the time (5 percent of the time this equipment is not available due to breakdowns or planned shutdown). If the production on this equipment was 97 percent of the maximum production rate that this equipment has consistently made earlier, the production efficiency is 97 percent. Let's assume 99 percent of the production on this equipment could be sold (1 percent was wasted). Then OEE of this equipment is estimated to be 0.95 x 0.97 x 0.99 or 0.91 (91%). An OEE of greater than 85 percent in most industries is considered world-class. If OEE is running lower than expected, one can identify from the OEE formula which factor is not meeting its target and accordingly can engage the right people or team to address the issue of poor performance.

A world-class operation will use online process control tools and methods to optimise its processes. A manufacturing business must embrace digital transformation in this day and age. Operation and maintenance personnel with real-time data on their machines and processes can make better decisions on whether they should make any changes to their equipment or processes based on the data. Automation of processes can make real-time adjustments to the process (to valves, pumps, and fans) so processes are optimised constantly. Maintenance personnel can plan maintenance based on online vibration, temperature, or motor data. Digital tools will monitor asset health online and alert the key personnel, if there are some concerns and if any actions are warranted.

Process or production engineers can closely monitor process trends and address any process variance that could result in lower production efficiency rates or quality yields. A world-class operation will have a highly coordinated team in production, process, quality, and maintenance. This team will come together as needed and address any issues of concern. The team will review OEE and other relevant trends and performance parameters regularly and initiate prompt actions as needed. Also, relevant trends and charts of key performance indicators (KPIs) will be posted for other employees to view. Individual departments must go over these KPIs with their staff and engage them proactively in addressing any issues of concern. A culture of operational excellence will be created, and the site will continue to see continuous improvements in its performance. A good performance will boost the morale of the employees and help build a culture of pride and engagement.

7.10 Practice Operational Excellence and Go Beyond

As we said earlier in the operational excellence chapter, it is very important to strive for operational excellence (i.e., optimise the processes and system as a whole); however, we must not stop at it. In operational excellence, we eliminate "waste" by maximizing output and minimizing waste (or minimizing input), and as a result, we aim to maximise the margin of the business. (A waste is anything in the process that does not add value).

While operation excellence is a must, the site or the business though not stop just on operation excellence and must invest enough in innovation, so it is not left behind and become a victim of creative destruction.

7.11 Must Do Data Analysis for Good Insight and Decisions

A point of caution here, we have observed many production supervisors or managers lack statistical knowledge to be able to analyse the useful data available to them from their processes. This data provides insight into processes, and aid in understand why certain process behave in certain ways when there are changes in some input parameters. Process engineers and production personnel must be trained in statistics so they can perform relevant statistical analysis and decide what actions, if any.

7.12 Embrace Sustainable Development

Another important point is that future senior leaders of the business must be trained on environmental issues (site-specific, industry-specific, and global issues such as climate change) and sustainable development. They must be exposed to community issues as well and must be active enough in their local communities, so communities know them and can trust them. Remember, communities can oppose the permits that you receive from the local or federal government, which can create lots of issues for your site. Leaders and managers must build a trustworthy relationship with communities and stay honest and transparent (follow SD principles). These leaders also must be trained on the basics of finances (and this is the reason we have included a whole section on finances in this book). They must know what balance sheet, income statement, and cash flow statement carry and why they are important to businesses. They must know what cost is your regular expense and what can be capitalised. They must know enough about how capital expenditure or high inventories of raw materials, products, or spare parts affect their cash flow. Why just EBIT is not enough to understand how a site is doing? Why a certain return on investment must be expected on a certain investment (why just a positive return is not good enough. Rather the mindset of operation managers most times is to rely heavily on the finance department to analyse these reports and advise production, maintenance, and process personnel. While heavy reliance on the finance department may manage the situation to some extent, however, I believe the lack of knowledge or interest in understanding the basics of the finance side of the business hurt the operation and overall performance of the site. Aspiring non-finance leaders, in manufacturing, must make themselves knowledgeable of the basics of finance. With this knowledge and its application, they will be much more effective and influential leaders.

The point is these current and future senior leaders of the company must be good economic thinkers and relate business decisions to financial outcomes. Of course, good leaders and managers must go beyond the financial impact and consider environmental and social impacts of their decisions.

There are many operation tools that, I believe, will be highly useful to current as well as new leaders and managers. A summary of these tools is provided in the next chapter. I encourage all managers and leaders to use these tools and encourage your team to use them to become a more effective team and better leaders individually.

8

Take Care of Customers

For good customer care, we must first understand what our customers want from us. What their metric is for us? Is it the turn-around time on an order? Is it the cost they care about the most? Or is it the product's appearance and quality? Some customers may want consistency in product quality and product performance. Big fluctuations, in quality, even if the quality parameters are within specs, may still cause pain to customers. We must also understand clearly what product quality means to our customers. Product quality could mean meeting all engineering and regulatory specs to manufacturing engineers and quality personnel. What customers mean by product quality may be product appearance, dependability, and ease of operation. Furthermore, a customer may require 24×7 fast and reliable service to address any unplanned downtime due to our products.

The point is that customers do not just want physical products, they want to have a good experience also with anything to do with our products and services. After having clarity on what customers want from us, we then must work backward and identify any gaps in our system (e.g., process fluctuations, technology gaps, digital constraints, equipment reliability, and lack of customer service support) that may hinder us to fulfill our commitment to customers. After identifying these gaps, we must then prioritise our actions to eliminate (or reduce their adverse impacts on our customer commitment) the most important gaps in the process and remove those gaps promptly to consistently provide a great customer experience. Unless our management system, operation processes, and management support are synced and fully prepared to meet customer commitment consistently, we cannot deliver a great customer experience. At best, it will be a hit-and-miss type of experience. We may have great equipment and technology; however, if our management processes are confusing, cumbersome, and bureaucratic, customer care will not be consistent. We will continue to struggle in meeting our commitments to customers. Poor leadership and low employee morale will not allow us to continue striving for excellence in customer experience. An engaged workforce is key to a great customer experience. Employees are the ones who will identify and fix the issues associated with our equipment, management processes, quality system, and technology-related issues. An engaged workforce can develop customer empathy which is essential in establishing a customer-care culture.

Customer Care Evolution: One hundred years back, we will be happy to travel long distances to get the products we wanted. We were willing to wait for long if the product was not available. Once we purchased the product and it had some faults, we did not have the luxury to call the company by phone. The company will not necessarily send a service person to fix their product. We will write complaint letters explaining our issue with the product quality. If we were lucky, we will get a response back with a possible resolution to our problem. The alternative will be to have the product (part or equipment) returned the supplier or manufacturer ourselves and have it fixed or replaced.

Technological innovation changed this way of customer and manufacturer interaction. Telephones came into being and were available to the public. Some fifty to sixty years ago, companies started to install switchboards to handle customer calls and publish their customer service numbers for customers to call if they had issues. The customer "experience" improved quite a bit, as customers did not have to write letters and wait for a long time for responses. With the invention of the internet in the late twentieth century, instant messaging and emails became available to customers and their heavy reliance on the landline phone decreased to interact with product or service providers. In the last two decades, social platforms evolved. Customers had easy access to compare different product and service offerings. Internet search allowed customers to search for the best quality products at good prices. Customers could read online reviews of products and services. Customers could have live chats with company representatives. Customers could make their issues public online on social media, forcing responsible companies to act swiftly to address any issues or concerns. Customers now had better control of their situation and were not at the mercy of product manufacturers or providers.

Several companies such as Amazon, FedEx, Apple, and Google have taken the customer experience to new heights. Amazon can deliver the products to our doorsteps in twenty-four hours. If we are not satisfied with the product or the product is lost, Amazon will replace the product promptly. Customers can order their products online with great ease. The company provides several choices of similar products for us to choose from based on quality, price, or appearance. FedEx delivers products the next day. Customers can track their shipments online. Apple has redefined product quality and product experience to an imaginable level by providing elegant phones with highly useful features. Google's Alexa can follow our commands and play music, tell jokes, or set the room's thermostat temperature.

Companies are currently experimenting with the use of artificial intelligence and developing predictive intelligence tools to take customer experience to the next level. Companies are tracking consumers online with their spending habits and lifestyle choices and collecting data on their income and assets. Based on this information and data analytics, companies are getting ready to take customer experience to the next level (the company proactively can offer us products and services that we value and may not be aware that great options were available to us).

With fast-changing technological innovations, customers expect ease of doing business further along with reliable, relevant, and consistent product and services in a swift manner. With the internet and today's technology, it is easy for customers to shop around for products and services at competitive prices. In the fast-changing technological world and with growing customers' expectations, we must take the following actions to ensure we stay relevant and reliable and continue to provide a great customer experience.

- *Provide great product experience*: It means we must have a quality product with consistency. The quality must be in line with what the customer wants. The product must perform as expected. The product must meet the on-time delivery commitment.
- *Provide great service experience*: It means fast, friendly, and caring service to customers across the organisation (be it field service, customer service support, and interaction with finance personnel). The entire organisation must be in sync with customer-centric values, so, the customer has a consistent experience with all touchpoints in the organisation.
- *Use digital technology to make operation and business processes robust to support customer-centric culture*: To provide consistent quality products and services, we must have a reliable operation with good support from engineering and quality. The culture of the organisation must be such that any issues that may impact customer experience adversely must be addressed promptly. Similarly, business processes must be simplified to support the customer experience. Digital technology must provide ease of customer interaction with us (in ordering products, checking the status of their product in the manufacturing process, shipping process, getting in contact with customer service with ease, and so forth).
- *Train workforce on customer interaction and customer-centric culture*: A lot is being said in the business world about creating a customer-centric culture. However, employees

are not trained on what it means to be customer-centric and how to become one. A customer-centric organisation will train its workforce on customer care and experience, and encourage everybody to relate their work to customer care and their experience. Employees coming in frequent contact with customers must be trained in customer communication to feel confident while dealing with customers and make them feel listened to and respected. These employees must be trained on how to build long-lasting relationships with customers. We must never forget human contact is the most important aspect of customer experience. We like people who are trustworthy, genuine, confident, and caring. Employees in the organisation must be trained on how to build a win-win relationship with customers.

In summary, for great customer experience, we must deliver a great quality product consistently and meet our on-time delivery commitment. Our customer service must be fast, friendly, and caring. The individual parts of an organisation must support customer-centric culture and be in sync with one another. Our production processes must be reliable and consistent. Our business processes must be simple and customer friendly. Our employees must be trained in customer care and have full awareness of how their work is helping enhance customer experience. An engaging workforce will enable great customer experience by delivering great product experience and service experience to customers.

Our manufacturing technology as well as digital technology must support the current and future customer experience expectations. If we fail to upgrade our manufacturing technology or digital technology to support a great customer experience, we will risk being irrelevant and may be a victim of a powerful, creative destructive force. Finally, we must be trustworthy, respectful, and fair to customers and always think to build a win-win, long-term relationship with customers. A one-sided approach (a selfish approach) will surely put our business on the path of destruction (a monopoly also may survive for some time only; new entrants in the market will again force us to be customer-centric for the long-term success of our business). A win-win approach co-creates a much larger value in the market than a selfish approach. A win-win approach will also create a great customer experience as well.

9

Highly Useful Tools for Operations Leaders

A variety of management tools are used in manufacturing and process industries to stay proactive or address an issue at hand or do an after-action review for further actions. In my leadership journey in different industries, I have found the following tools to be of high value for leaders and managers in their operational excellence journey. These tools when used sincerely by the staff add a lot of value to our business. The tools can be used by any business or operation as such and are not limited to the manufacturing industry only. A summary of each tool is presented in the following sections.

9.1 Failure Mode Effect Analysis—a Powerful Method for All Manufacturing Sites

Failure mode effect analysis (FMEA) is a qualitative, systematic, and powerful tool to predict likely failures in the process, equipment, or equipment components. FMEA method was originally developed in the 1940s by the US military (www.asq.org). ASQ is the American Society of Quality). This method identifies failure modes, causes of failures, likely frequencies of these failures, and the severity of these failures on business (e.g., what will be the likely impact on a customer, what will be the revenue loss

Table 9.1: FMEA Template

Equipment Sub-Systems	Failure Modes	Cause	Probability (P) or Frequency of Occurence	Effect (or Severity S)	S	P	Assumptions / E	Recommendations
								ACTION TAKEN
Motor	Synchronous starter fails	fuses blow up	Once Every 5 years	45 minutes + 1 day produc	III	E	No fuses in stock	Keep 3 fuses in stock.
		Transformer fails		6 hours + 3 days	I	E		
		Power cables burns	Once Every 20 years or	2 and half days	II	F		
		Loose connections		2 hours	IV	E		
		Excessive dirts		2 months	I	E		
		Overheating due to a failure of AC		2 hours	IV	D		
		SPM controller fails		2 months	I	F	Obsolete	
		PLC communication lost		2 hours	IV	E		
		Accidently emergency button pushed		1 hour	IV	E		
	Bearing failure	Wrong lubrication	Once Every 5 years	3 weeks to re-built	I	E		stock. Oil analysis is performed. Inspection checklist has to be

due to a given failure mode). The failure mode is one of the possible defects in the process, equipment, or system component. Failure modes direct us to the root cause(s) of these failure modes and lead us to actions to eliminate the associated causes that might result in failure modes.

In this method, a team is formed with the right people who have a good understanding of the process, equipment, or components. It is always a great idea that the team is diverse in skills and experiences and be very open and honest in their discussion while working on FMEAs. The team assigns a risk factor or risk category to each possible cause and then prioritises them based on overall risk. A risk can be defined as the probability of occurrence multiplied by a score assigned to the severity of a particular occurrence. Probability is associated with the frequency of occurrence of the identified cause while severity is the adverse impact the failure will cause to the business (in terms of revenue loss, operation loss, or impact to customer). A severity score is identified based on the gravity of the adverse impact.

To illustrate how we use FMEA, Table 9.1 presents a simple scenario of failure modes on a piece of equipment at an imaginary manufacturing site.

Note that in the above scenario, probability and severity are identified for each cause associated with the failure mode. One of the methods then is to develop a risk matrix based on this information and place the overall risk visually on the two-dimensional matrix. The team can assign colours (e.g., red means unacceptable risk, yellow means the risk is in the warning category, and green means not high risk and so acceptable) to each risk grid which captures severity and probability information. A risk matrix is illustrated in Table 9.2.

Table 9.2: A Two-Dimensional Risk Matrix with Probability and Severity

Risk Matrix

Probability					
	A - Very high (once per 3 months)	A - Very high (once per 3 months)			
	B - Moderate (once per 6 months)				
	C - Occasional (once per 1 year)				
	D - Remote (once per 2 to 3 years)				
	E - Unlikely (once per 5 years)				
	F - Impossible (once per 20 yrs.)				
		IV : Negligible	III : Moderate	II : High	I : Catastrophic
		Severity			

Operation loss From [days]:	0 to 3	3 to 5	5 to 13.5	over 13.5 [days]
Revenue Lost [kUSD]:	0 - 621	621 - 1035	1035 - 2795	over 2795
Maintenance cost [kUSD]:	0 - 25	26 - 100	101 - 600	over 601

Note that the team has defined severity based on operation loss, revenue loss, and maintenance cost. Probability is assigned in letters as A, B, C, D, E, or F based on the frequency of the failure (cause that resulted in failure). The team has the freedom to customise these criteria of probability and severity and build the matrix based on their agreed-upon guidelines. Once the risk matrix is defined and the grids are coloured in advance, the identified scenarios can be placed on this matrix. The team can focus on red scenarios first and initiate appropriate actions so these scenarios can be turned from red to yellow as much as possible and cost-effectively. Scenarios associated with yellow boxes may require a lesser degree of attention.

In the above FMEA matrix, bearing failure was identified as having a probability category of C and a severity category of I. It means the bearing failure may happen once every year, and if it happens, it will cause catastrophic conditions due to an operational loss of 13.5 days (as the bearing is special and has a long lead time), a revenue loss of more than $2.7 million, and maintenance cost of greater than $600,000. The risk colour on the risk matrix assigned to this particular failure mode and cause is red. The team must take some drastic actions to prevent this failure from happening. It means lubrication sampling may be done frequently, lubrication PM must be ensured, and the site may want to have this bearing on hand as well to mitigate the risk.

Other than developing the risk matrix in the FMEA method, the other method is to assign a risk priority number (RPN), which is a numeric assessment of risk assigned to the particular failure (cause of the failure) in a process. One such FMEA sheet is provided in Table 9.2 (modified from the asq.org sheet).

The team assigns a numeric code to the likelihood of occurrence (probability in the above matrix), the severity of impact, and the likelihood of detection. Note that the detection rating estimates how well the current controls can detect either the failure or the cause of the failure mode after they have happened (before the failure has affected the customer). The three numeric codes are multiplied to get the RPN score for each cause of the failure mode. The numeric

Table 9.3: FMEA with Risk Priority Number

FAILURE MODE AND EFFECTS ANALYSIS

Item:	Drill Hole	Responsibility:	J. Doe
Model:	Current	Prepared by:	J. Doe
Core Team:	Engineering, Maintenance, Operation Personnel		

Process Function	Potential Failure Mode	Potential Effect(s) of Failure	Sev	Potential Cause(s)/ Mechanism(s) of Failure	Occurrence	Current Process Controls	Detection	RPN	Recommended Action(s)
Drill Blind Hole	Hole too deep	Break through bottom of plate	7	Improper machine set up	3	Operator training and instructions	3	63	
	Hole not deep enough	Incomplete thread form	5	Broken Drill	5	Operator training and instructions	9	225	Install Tool Detectors

codes can be any numbers assigned by the team (e.g., 1–5, 1–10, etc.). Note that if a particular failure cause can be detected relatively easily before the failure really occurs, a lower numeric value will be assigned to the detection score (so when this score is multiplied by the probability of occurrence and severity of occurrence, it lowers the RPN score). The ultimate goal of this approach is to reduce the RPN score of different failure modes below an acceptable level by taking actions (e.g., maintenance PMs, walk-by inspections, predictive maintenance, and keeping spare parts in inventory if necessary). In the above example, if after the tool detector is installed, the detection score says it now dropped from 9 to 3, the overall RPN score will reduce to 75.

The FMEA method is a powerful tool available to managers to use proactively and initiate actions to mitigate identified risks associated with a process, function, equipment, or subsystems. In addition, FMEA is a great tool to use to optimise spare parts inventories at manufacturing sites. This method will guide leaders and managers on what spare parts to keep in inventory and what not (based on agreed-upon accepted risk criteria) and thus optimise their inventory and manage this key cash flow item appropriately. Most often, operating managers, front-line supervisors, and engineers are needed to participate in the FMEAs. Many times, site personnel have numerous responsibilities and may have difficulty allocating time for this exercise. Our suggestion for the site leadership is to work with them, educate them, and inspire them to participate even if it is done in phases per a planned schedule over a few months to a year or two depending on the complexities of the operation. However, the commitment must be that it will certainly be done per an agreed-upon timeline. The business can develop a competitive edge once this analysis is performed and its recommendations are implemented.

9.2 Fishbone Diagram for Root Cause Analysis

The fishbone diagram, also known as the Ishikawa diagram, is a visual and highly effective technique for problem-solving. This technique was invented by Kaoro Ishikawa, a Japanese quality control expert. To use this technique effectively, a team is formed and the problem is defined carefully. The team must consist of the right people who are aware of the operation, equipment, process, or issue being faced.

In this technique, the likely causes of the problem are identified into any of the following categories: manpower, machine, method, materials, measurements, and environment (5 Ms and 1 E—just to remember). Note that these categories are the ones that are most likely to capture the identified causal factors for a given problem. It means once a problem has surfaced that forces us to look into the problem deeper, we must look for causal factors in these categories and ask questions if something significant has changed in any of these categories resulting in the problem that we are facing now. A causal factor is an issue that if corrected could have prevented the problem from occurring or significantly reduced the problem's consequences, the visual method (see the attached fishbone diagram in the side exhibit) is very powerful and guides the team intuitively to separate the likely causes into different categories.

The team, while using the fishbone method, can even apply the 5-why technique to each identified causal factor to determine the root cause(s) of the problem and can recommend actions to prevent the likely cause(s) to occur again.

Let's take an example to show how we use this technique. A manufacturing site repairs engine components and monitors the turn-around time (TAT) of these parts as the TAT is important to customers. Lately, it has been observed that the TAT of some key components has increased significantly. Now let's use the fishbone method to analyse the issue and drill down deeper.

The fishbone diagram in Figure 9.1 shows the likely causal factors in each category and encourages the team to check physically if the identified causal factor has really happened and if yes then the team may use the 5-why method to get to the root cause of that causal factor. For the TAT problem here, we suspect a shortage of manpower due to some retirements that took place lately (assumptions), and we lost expertise to repair the particular part of the concern. One

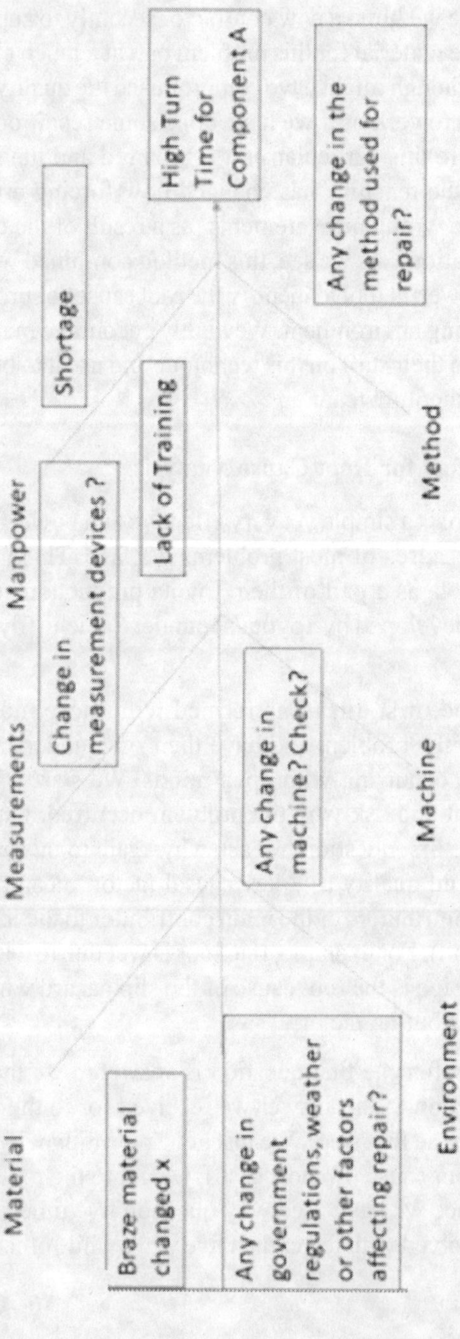

Fig. 9.1: The Fishbone Diagram.

can also determine we hired a new contractor recently to supply us with the new braze material for this problem part at a much cheaper rate. This change though might have compromised the quality of the repair resulting in rework or if we have done some repair on some key machine where this particular part is repaired and the setting or calibration of the machine has changed now forcing errors in repairs now due to wrong measurements (as a result of the change in machine calibration). As we see, this method combined with the 5-why can be a powerful tool to identify the root causes of problems in the manufacturing environment. We highly encourage managers and leaders to train their staff on this technique and use it to become a smarter troubleshooting team.

9.3 The 5-Why Tool for Root Cause Analysis

The 5-why tool is a simple yet very effective and powerful tool to get to the root causes of most problems we face. This method originated in Toyota as a part of their Toyota production system. The method was developed by Toyota's founder Sakichi Toyoda in the early 1930s.

In this method, first a team is formed with those members who are aware of the problem and have their own understanding of what might be occurring with open minds. We start with the problem statement and ask why the problem occurred. Once we have answered the first question, we ask why again to this answer. This response could qualify as a key causal factor, meaning it is one of the main contributors or the main contributor to the incident (or problem at hand). For example, if a floor is wet due to a leaking pipe, the leaking pipe is the root cause of the slip hazard while the wet floor is a contributing factor.

Furthermore, after the first question is answered we then ask another why question to the answer we received (or to the causal factor identified in the first step). We just keep repeating whys until we uncover the root cause. In most cases, we get to the root cause of the problem once we have used why question five times. Some problems can be solved with fewer than five whys while others may take additional whys. It is very likely a problem may have more than one causal factor. The 5-why method should be applied to all causal factors to get to the root causes of these causal factors. We should recommend solutions that will address the identified root causes of the problem or eliminate the causal factors.

While the 5-why is a powerful and effective tool to determine the root cause of simple to moderate levels of complex problems, there are many other sophisticated tools to perform the root cause analysis for complex problems. Two of these useful methods include the fishbone (or Ishikawa) diagram and failure mode and effect analysis (FMEA) and were discussed in earlier sections. In these methods also, causal factors are identified to uncover the root cause(s). We can still apply the 5-why tool to these causal factors to get to the root causes of those causal factors.

Let's consider the following two examples and apply the 5-why tool to identify the root causes of the problem at hand.

Problem 1: The swimming pool pump is not pumping water.

The team (maybe you are the team in this case or you have your friend who has good knowledge of swimming pool pumps and circulating systems) first identifies the most probable, say, three causal factors. These causal factors include the pool inlet diffuser blocking the inlet of the impeller, the pool suction side having some restrictions, and the pool suction side having some air leaks. Now let's apply five whys to each of these causal factors.

Five Whys on Causal Factors

Causal Factor 1:

1. Why is the diffuser blocking the inlet (center) of the impeller?

   Response: Diffuser dislocated.

   Why is the diffuser dislocated?

   Response: The diffuser's one of the two screws found broken.
2. Why is the diffuser screw broken?

Response: Old design of diffuser for this pump.

Recommendation: Check and fix the inlet diffuser (if displaced) by replacing the broken screw.

Causal Factor 2:

1. Why is the suction line restricting the water flow?

   Response: The isolation valve in the suction line is blocking the skimmer and pool drain lines partially.

2. Why is the isolation valve restricting the skimmer and pool drain lines?

   Response: The valve is not installed properly.

3. Why is the valve not installed properly?

   Response: Unknown reason.

Recommendation: Check and fix the valve on the suction line if restricting flow or replace it with a new one.

Causal Factor 3:

1. Why is the suction line having an air leak?

   Response: The vacuum line (pool to the pump inlet) has cracks.

2. Why does the vacuum line have cracks?

   Response: Old line (regular worn out due to aging).

Recommendation: Replace or block this line (not needed as the pool is vacuumed manually or with an automatic pool cleaner).

Problem 2: The dust collector is not able to operate. In this problem, we have asked the why question and identified one main causal factor in response to question 2. One could start five whys with the question why the fan belt broke? We may get to the root cause for a give causal factor in fewer than five whys or sometimes it may take more than five whys as well.

1. Why is the dust collector not able to operate?

   Response: The fan of the dust collector will not run.

2. Why will the fan not run?

   Response: The fan belt broke.

3. Why did the fan belts break?

   Response: Belts ran out of their service life

4. Why did fan belts run out of their service life?

   Response: No new belts in the store room to replace.

5. Why are there no belts in the storeroom to replace?

   Response: No minimum quantity was identified in the inventory management programme.

Recommendations: Identify the minimum number of belts in inventory and order these belts (expedite) and replace them as soon as possible.

9.4 The Checklist

Using a checklist in some special, complex scenarios to prevent big mistakes is a very simple yet very powerful idea. We highly recommend managers and leaders encourage the use of checklists in a complex environment where people may have too many distractions. Checklists, if used correctly, can save lives and make operations less vulnerable to mistakes. In a complex work environment, even experts are subject to the fallibility of human memory and attention. Mundane, routine matters may be overlooked under a strain of higher priority issues.

Dr. Atul Gawande, MD, has written the *New York Times* bestseller, *The Checklist Manifesto* on this very subject and has provided numerous examples of how checklists are used in aviation, surgical procedures, and the construction industry. Airlines use checklists not only for preflight checks but also for different emergencies that may cause catastrophic conditions if certain situations are not handled correctly. Airlines have found these checklists very useful and pilots and flight engineers use them regularly throughout the world. These checklists are very simple and contain a few lines for different emergency scenarios. WHO initiated a checklist programme for hospitals to use during surgical procedures basic, yet critical steps are not missed which could lead to major complications or death. According to the WHO, after the simple checklists are used by medical staff in the operating rooms of eight hospitals around the world, the final results show major complications dropped by 36 percent and the death toll fell by 47 percent. Close to 80 percent of 250 surgeons, anesthesiologists, nurses, and others reported these checklists which are easy to use, required very little time to complete, and improved the safety of the procedures. These checklists consisted of reminders to conduct a team "introduction" and to briefly discuss critical aspects of a given case. This improves teamwork and communication. The checklist will also have the patient's identity to make sure the team had the right patient in the operating room. Also, the checklist reminds the operating team to wash their hands with soap, wear their surgical gowns, and wear masks to avoid any infection spreading and hurting the patients during the procedure.

The anesthesia checklist had seven checks. One of these checks was to check the patient's medication allergies. The reminder is to check for any airway issues. Another check was to verify if necessary intravenous lines, blood, and fluids are ready in case the patient loses more than half a liter of blood. The point is these checklists were simple, yet had critical reminders some of which at times even smart doctors and their staff may forget due to so many distractions as well complexities involved in their work.

Similarly in the process industry, checklists are used by proactive teams and management for critical checks by operators and engineers. Without the use of these checklists in certain situations, serious mistakes do happen to cause equipment breakdowns, process failures, quality issues, or safety problems. When starting a process line, if all key equipment is not ready or the supporting equipment is feeding the corrective chemical is not ready (not calibrated or started using it without calibration), we risk failing critical equipment or making a substandard product due to the possibility of using incorrect measurement of the corrective mixture in the process. If another downstream piece of equipment was not ready, and the upstream equipment was started due to lack of communication or lack of checks, the process line may develop critical issues (material being fed by upstream equipment but the downstream equipment is not ready to transfer it) such as material spillage, material buildup, or overflow of harmful chemical to the ground. These conditions may also cause process hazards and compromise the safety of people in the work area. For emergency scenarios, even well-trained operators may make mistakes due to various distractions or complexities of the process.

An observation we have from the manufacturing industry is people's reluctance to use these checklists if they do not see their value. Hence, it is important when developing these checklists to engage operators who will be using them and seek their input.

Also, we must remember there are good checklists and bad checklists. Atul Gawande has provided some guidelines Bad checklists are long, too detailed, are full of clutter, and their format is not user-friendly. Good checklists are precise, short (one pager and not more than nine lines if possible as this is the limit of working memory), and easy to use. Checklists must have only key reminders. As our memories and judgments are unreliable and people's lives may depend on our decisions, it is crucial we provide only critical points on checklists that people may forget. In emergencies, pilots and flight engineers rely more on their checklists rather than their instincts to address the situation, and that too in a very short period.

9.5 Management of Change (MOC) for Non-Routine Changes

The management of change (MOC) procedure is a tool to ensure non-routine changes in manufacturing are reviewed, approved, documented, and communicated properly to the affected employees or stakeholders. The MOC process helps mitigate costly mistakes or incidents from happening due to its emphasis on communication among stakeholders. The MOC process was originally implemented by OSHA after a serious accident at the Union Carbide plant in Bhopal, India, in 1984, killing close to 3,000 people.

The following template is just an example of how a template similar to the one below can be used to manage the MOC process. The template may be customised to suit your specific process or operation.

Management of Change (MOC)

Example Template

The management of change (MOC) procedure is a tool to ensure non-routine changes in manufacturing are reviewed, approved, documented, and communicated properly to the affected employees or stakeholders. The MOC process helps mitigate costly mistakes or incidents from happening due to its emphasis on communication among stakeholders.

Name of Originator:______________________________

Department:______________________________

Date of Request:__________

Type of Nonroutine Change (Check all that apply)

Process (All except machining)

Machining

EHS/Environment

Manpower/Organisation

Lab/Other Methods

Brief description of the proposed change and why:

____

Follow-up actions which must be taken as a result of this change

____

Approvers: Check departments that must approve (Dept. head or delegate must sign)

Operations

Quality

Engineering

Maintenance

Operations

Communication: Check all departments that must receive notification of this change

Operations

Finance

Supervisors

Quality

Human Resources

All Site Employees

Engineering

Supply Chain

General Manager

Customer Service

EHS

Effective date of change:

Originator of Change (Print Name):

Signature & Date:

9.6 SWOT Analysis

Strength, weakness, opportunity, and threat (SWOT) analysis is a good tool to identify the strengths and weaknesses of your business as well as recognise opportunities and threats in the business environment. It should be noted while strengths and weaknesses are internal to the business, opportunities and threats are external. It is highly recommended a team with the right players with a good understanding of operation and business perform the SWOT analysis. The team members must be open-minded and go over the business's strengths and weaknesses as well as opportunities and threats facing the business.

SWOT Analysis - Hypothetical Site

Strength	Opportunity
Repeat Business Experienced workforce Great work condition (environment, schedule) Core Comptencies: State of the art machines Raw material easy availability Rail and Road Transportation	New Technologies (can be industralized) New Business Opportunities/ Ventures New Products Sustainability
Weakness	**Threats**
Aging workforce/ Retirements Workforce Engagement Low reliability of Operation equipment Training gaps Maintenance Program Capex Restrictions Old e-Management System (Software) Limited suppliers of key raw materials Operations and Sales Coordination	Emerging Technologies Tight Labor markets Sustainability Global business environment (Wars, Disease)

Fig. 9.2: SWOT Analysis Example.

After the SWOT matrix as shown in Figure 9.2 is developed, the team then must come up with an action plan with specific actions that can allow the business to take advantage of key opportunities available in the market. At the same time, the team must address any major threats that may have a significant impact on the business if the threat really happens. For example, if the opportunity is to develop new products, the business may decide to realign resources so some resources can be dedicated to new product development. If a threat to the business is some emerging technology, the business must consider accelerating its adoption of new technology. The business must pay attention to its weaknesses also and identify those weaknesses that will harm the business to a great deal if not taken care of currently. For example, a weak maintenance programme will eventually hurt the business significantly as the machines will start breaking down frequently due to poor maintenance and preventive maintenance practices. A good maintenance programme will help improve the reliability of the operation and the morale of the people. Furthermore, if there are only a few raw material suppliers, the business may want to look for new suppliers to dilute its risk of having a few suppliers for raw materials.

SWOT analysis is a great tool to allow businesses to recognise their strengths, weaknesses, threats, and opportunities and subsequently come up with an action plan to address issues associated with business weaknesses or market threats and opportunities based on priorities.

9.7 Porter's Five Force Analysis for Business Strategy

Business leaders and managers have an interest in running not only day-to-day business but also formulating the long-term strategy for their business. Whether you are in a business strategy group or are directly or indirectly providing input to the leadership regarding how business must be shaped for the future, you will find Porter's model highly useful in analyzing the market forces that may impact your business in the future. This model brings a lot of clarity to your own thinking once you use it for your business with your key team players. I will highly recommend to new managers and leaders that they have a basic understanding of this model.

Prof. Michael Porter of Harvard University discovered and published this model in *Harvard Business Review* in March 1979. Michael Porter identified five market forces that are always there and will have a small or big impact on your business depending on the strengths of these forces in your industry. These five forces are exhibited in the diagram below (Figure 9.3).

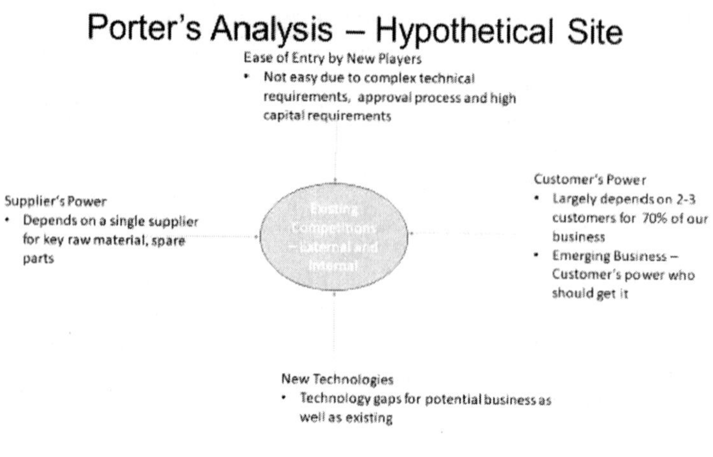

Fig. 9.3: Porter's Five Forces Diagram

As shown in the diagram, the five forces include the possibility of new entrants, customer power, new technologies, supplier power, and existing competition in the industry. Either the collective strength of these forces or the strongest individual force will determine how profitable your business will be in the future and what kind of upwind force(s) the business may have to face. By analyzing each force and the strengths and weaknesses of your business, you may decide if you must take further actions to mitigate the negative impact of any or all of these forces. For example, if a new player can have an easy entry into your industry, this poses a possible threat to your business and may hurt your profitability. Similarly, if suppliers have lots of power over your business (e.g., supplier of unique raw materials which only this supplier can sell you), your profitability can be affected, and the business risk can be high due to just having a single supplier. Emerging technologies will also act like a gale force unless you have embraced new technologies proactively (or your business can be a victim of creative destruction). If your business depends only on a few customers, your customers then your business may have a huge adverse impact on your profitability. In this situation, it is better to diversify and add many more customers to your portfolio. Other than the four external forces, the fifth one is internal from other competitors in your own industry. Your competition may introduce new products, have price competition, spend a lot on marketing and advertisement campaigns, and make you less competitive in the market. Leaders and managers will benefit by analyzing these five forces, identifying the strengths and weaknesses of their own businesses, and taking timely actions to shape the strategy for their business to stay competitive in the industry.

9.8 The 80-20 Rule

The 80-20 rule is also referred to as the Pareto principle after Italian economist Vilfredo Pareto, who observed it for the first time in 1896 in his backyard while growing pea plants. Based on his observation, 20 percent of his pea plants generated 80 percent of healthy pea pods. During this time, he made another observation in the society at large that 80 percent of the land in Italy was owned by 20 percent of the population.

This rule is very powerful and helps us prioritise our time and resources. The rule seems to be universal and applies to most things in life we observe around us. For example, in the manufacturing world, this is a general observation universally that 80 percent of machine or production line failures are caused by 20 percent causes. In workplaces, 80 percent of work injuries are caused by 20 percent of work hazards. Globally, 80 percent of the country's income is in the hands of 20 percent of its population. Similarly, it is mostly accepted in the business world that 80 percent of sales are caused by 20 percent of salespeople. Again, 80 percent of business revenue might be coming from 20 percent of its products. One study (Dunedin) has found that 80 percent of crimes are caused by 20 percent of criminals.

In our work or life, if we are mindful of this rule and prioritise our time and resources to address those 20 percent factors that are influencing 80 percent of our work, we will be more productive and efficient and enjoy our work and life better.

In manufacturing, a technical team consisting of engineers, maintenance personnel, and operation and quality staff collect and analyse lots of data and can show on charts how more or less than 20 percent of issues are causing 80 percent of the problem. Similarly, quality professionals can show by way of presenting data in chart forms how 80 percent of quality issues are caused by 20 percent of factors. This seems to be the case universally in manufacturing. One such chart is called the Pareto chart. In this chart, one can show frequencies of different failures of the machine or production line and their respective causes. Based on this chart, the team will focus on only the top 20 percent of contributing factors that will cause 80 percent failures.

9.9 The 4-Way Test

(A Powerful Tool for Win-Win Relationships)

I have been a member of Rotary International for fourteen years.

I am really impressed with one of the tools that Rotary International uses to build winning relationships with all those who we interact with. Most Rotary meetings worldwide will end with the 4-way test, and all members will say it together. This tool is a test, which is called the 4-way test. Basically, the test has four questions as below to ask of the things we think, say, or do.

1. Is it the truth?
2. Is it fair to all concerned?
3. Will it build goodwill and better friendships?
4. Will it be beneficial to all concerned?

The test is being used for the last seventy-five years by Rotary and many businesses successfully to build winning relationships with all stakeholders. How this test was developed has an interesting history. Chicago Rotarian Herbert J. Taylor was asked in 1932 to take charge of the Club Aluminum Products Company which was facing bankruptcy. The company had good cookware and a good brand name. The competition also had fine cookware and good recognition in the market and financially was stronger than Club Aluminum. Herbert J. Taylor quickly realised he must change the company culture so its employees build a win-win relationship with its customers, suppliers, contractors, and all other stakeholders. In the midst of the financial crisis of the company and the dire need to change, Herbert Taylor after some deep thinking and prayers came up with the 4-way test one fine morning.

The test was successfully applied by the Club Aluminum Company. The company culture changed shortly after the 4-way test was used by its employees in their daily dealing with one another and its stakeholders. As a result, the company regained the confidence and support of its customers and its financial health improved dramatically. Herbert Taylor gave the credit for the company's turnaround to the application of the 4-way test (clubrunner.blob.core.windows.net, en.wikipedia.org/wiki/ the-four-way-test, porter.clubrunner.ca).

The 4-way test was adopted by Rotary International in 1943. This test has been translated into more than one hundred languages and is one of the most widely printed and quoted statements of business ethics (clubrunner.blob.core.windows.net).

How to Use the 4-Way Test?

The purpose of the 4-way test is to ask these four questions about anything of high importance we think, say, or do. The first question, "Is it the truth" makes us think if the matter we have at hand is based on truth and facts and not on hearsay or our own biases. We must have hard evidence or data to prove what we are planning to do is really based on truth or facts. The second question, "Is it fair to all concerned?" ensures whatever we are planning to do is fair to not just one party rather it is fair to all key stakeholders (so we think win-win). The third question, "Will it build goodwill and better friendships?" takes our review of the situation one step further and encourages us to think about what we are planning to do and if we believe it will help build goodwill and better friendships. It means we have to go beyond our legal rights, or authority granted to us because of our position. We must think if our actions will help build goodwill (reputation, integrity, perception) and better friendships also. We are thus going beyond the legality of our actions. The fourth question, "Will it be beneficial to all concerned?" reinforces the point that we must check if our actions will be beneficial to all concerned. To build a win-win relationship, it is important we go beyond self and selfishness and create value for others.

It may be possible that in some unique scenarios, we may not have strong yes answers for all four questions. For example, if we have to discipline someone due to consistently poor performance, we can easily answer yes to each of the first two questions. When it comes to the third question, it may seem our action is not beneficial to the person being disciplined. However, if we pause for a minute, our action though may look tough will help this employee become a better employee (or at least give him or her an opportunity to become a better employee). The last question is if our action will be beneficial to all concerned beyond just the employee and the management in this case. The answer to question 4 is yes, our action will certainly motivate other employees on accountability (or they will be demoralised that we don't address issues at hand, in this case, the poor performance of a fellow associate).

The 4-way test, as such, is an ethical yardstick for us to use to monitor our thinking, language, and actions. The 4-way test can be applied at work and also in our homes and community as well. This way, we will become better sons, brothers, sisters, fathers, husbands, and friends. We will become good corporate citizens as well.

10

Concluding Remarks

As I conclude the writing of this book, I am immensely satisfied with the contents presented in the book. The book provides some powerful insights into key business matters and leadership aspects for young as well as seasoned leaders. The book has presented some basic yet very useful leadership lessons and tips that, once learned and applied, will empower aspiring leaders and managers. The book has brought diverse business and leadership know-how in a concise form in one place. Sustainable development, basic concepts of finances, macroeconomics, different leadership styles and motivation, operation excellence along with creative destruction, customer care, and important tools for operations leaders are included in the book. I believe, once the know-how presented in the book are learned and applied by young leaders and managers, they will be able to achieve stronger business results, build a culture where sustainable development concept is embraced, and employees are engaged and motivated for shared business vision, mission and goals.

I also trust this book will be of immense help to those who may not have easy access to leadership training and formal, academic study in a business programme (e.g., aspirants in developing or under-developed countries).

It is a great joy for me to present this book to all those who are motivated to take their leadership to the next level. I am confident the book will help them in their leadership growth with a quantum leap. I wish them all the best in their leadership journey.

Please share your comments about the book at kumar655@yahoo.com.

Book Review

1. I had the privilege to work side-by-side with Ajay and see him put into practice much of the knowledge he shares with you in his book "Leadership Journey: A Practical Guide for Quantum Leap to Your Leadership". If you're looking for a practical, down-to-earth guide to becoming a successful leader, I highly recommend you read Ajay's Journey.

   Steve Russo, President and CEO, Luma Sleep, USA

2. Regardless of your job experience level and the industry you work for, the golden nuggets of wisdom that you'll find throughout the book, will make a night and day difference, to your career and /or business, if fully grasped and deployed by you and your teams.

   Valentine (Val) De Jesus, Senior Operations Manager, Pratt and Whitney, USA

3. Regardless of your education or experience, readers of this book will benefit from learnings and concepts that will help them becoming successful in their P/L operations management journey. The novices will acquire a solid foundation in P/L operations management while the more experience ones will get a refresher on concepts we tend to forget over time.

   Maxime Labrecque, Vice President (MRO Operations) Pratt and Whitney Canada

4. If you are in an existing leadership role or that is your goal, you will most definitely want to read Ajay's book. It is very down to earth knowledge of how to be that successful leader. Being a Controller for years, I was very impressed with the Finance Chapter. In addition, I have had the pleasure of working for Ajay and I must say he "walks his talk" everyday!!.

   Dana Peterson, Site Controller
   Pratt and Whitney Canada, USA

5. This is an awesome, highly practical leadership book for both new and experienced leaders with great insights into highly critical areas (environment, finance, market, and people engagement) of the leadership of any business. I highly recommend this book to all current and future leaders from any business function such as Operations, Project Management, Human Resources, Finance, Customer Service or other areas. You will feel great and highly confident about yourself and your leadership skills once you have understood and applied the concepts presented in the book. A great practical book indeed on leadership!

   Udaibeer Singh, Manufacturing Business Owner,
   Dubai, UAE

6. I had the opportunity to work side by side with Ajay during the early part of our careers in the Fertilizer industry in India. Even at that time, I sensed some unique zeal in Ajay to positively contribute to society. Now I see that zeal culminating in the release of this book.

   All the key factors that ensure success are well explained in simple English, the method that easily connects with people and enables reading chapter after chapter without taking a break. Whether it is about sustainability and global warming or financial basics to non-financial managers or for that matter every subject he touched on here is well explained lucidly. I am glad Ajay allowed me to read this manuscript,

I feel privileged! I do not doubt in my mind, this book when it hits the stands will be the talk of current and future leaders across the globe!

M. N. Rao
Senior Vice President-Engineering
Aquatech International LLC
Canonsburg, PA 15317
USA

Index